OVERCOMING
THE ENEMY

OVERCOMING THE ENEMY

CHARLES STANLEY

THOMAS NELSON PUBLISHERS
Nashville • Atlanta • London • Vancouver

Published in Nashville, Tennessee, by Thomas Nelson, Inc., Publishers, and distributed in Canada by Word Communications, Ltd., Richmond, British Columbia, and in the United Kingdom by Word (UK), Ltd., Milton Keynes, England.

Scripture quotations are from THE NEW KING JAMES VERSION of the Bible. Copyright © 1979, 1980, 1982, Thomas Nelson, Inc., Publishers.

Scripture quotations noted KJV are from the KING JAMES VERSION.

ISBN 0-7852-7277-1

Printed in the United States of America

CONTENTS

CONTENTS

INTRODUCTION

OUR FOREMOST ENEMY

As believers in Christ Jesus we have three main enemies in life. They are constantly present to harass us, create conflict for us, and generate trouble for us. We cannot escape any of them completely as long as we are alive, although we are assured of victory over them as long as we rely on the Lord Jesus for our wisdom, power, and ability to endure.

Our three enemies are:

1. The world. The world includes anything of a physical nature that might hinder us in our walk with Christ or might tempt us to sin. Contrary to what some people think, the world is not getting better. If anything, it's getting worse because so many more possibilities related to evil exist today than existed hundreds or thousands of years ago—the world has more people, greater opportunities for evil alliances and evil behavior, more technology for delivering tempting messages, more access to weapons, more information about how to engage in evil, and more varieties of false religions. The ways and means for committing evil have exploded, not diminished.

2. The flesh. The nature of the human heart has not changed since the creation of human beings. The human heart still has a bent toward darkness, evil, and sin. We have desires, which God intends for us to meet in ways that are in keeping with His commandments. The temptation always exists, however, for us to seek to meet those desires in ways that are ungodly. Since we never lose our human, fleshly desires, we never lose our capacity to yield to temptation. These desires are with us until we die because they reside within us.

The devil. Peter describes our enemy this way:

"Your adversary the devil walks about like a roaring lion, seeking whom he may devour" (1 Peter 5:8).

Each of us faces a spiritual battle with the devil today whether we realize it or not. The very nature of the enemy of our eternal spirit is to defeat us, destroy us, and to kill everything that is important to us. His pursuit of us is persistent, unrelenting, and always aimed at the most vulnerable area of our lives.

A Need for Daily Victory

Because these three enemies are always with us, our best recourse is to learn how to deal with them and how to have daily victory over them. It would be wonderful if we could go on a fasting-and-prayer retreat and defeat the enemies once and for all in our lives, but that isn't a provision that God has made for us. Rather, He has provided us with the Holy Spirit who resides within us to help us in our struggle. The Holy Spirit gives us the ability to say no to the temptations of the world and to overcome and control our fleshly desires. The Holy Spirit also enables us to withstand the assaults of the devil on a day-to-day basis and to experience peace and wholeness even in the face of severe spiritual opposition.

We face a daily struggle. But we also can experience daily victories. Our Lord calls us to live one day at a time. We will not have a single, definitive showdown with the devil in our lives—a time in which he is defeated and will never come back to accuse or torment us again—but we can experience a *daily* victory over the devil. We can say no to the temptations he presents *today*. We can use our faith to defeat his assault against our minds, bodies, and spirits *today*. We can pray against his efforts to destroy us *today*. A string of daily victories makes for a victorious life!

Focusing on Our Spiritual Battle

We battle against the world and the flesh by learning first how to discern God's will and wisdom in a given situation or circumstance, and then how to have the courage and persevering power to say no to evil people, evil situations, and evil behavior. These battles are won or lost primarily on the battleground of our physical, material, relational, and emotional lives.

This study recognizes that we are engaged in an ongoing battle to overcome the world and the flesh, but it is based on the premise that the devil is behind these battles. Ultimately, our battle in each of these areas is spiritual in nature. It is waged "in the spirit," and it has eternal and far-reaching spiritual consequences.

The devil's purpose is not simply to irritate us or make our lives difficult. His goal is to destroy us in the spirit realm. The devil will use whatever is made available to him as a toehold on which to establish his evil purposes. His ultimate goal is to totally annihilate us—physically, materially, emotionally, mentally, and spiritually.

An Assurance of Victory

As we focus on spiritual warfare, we will do so from the perspective that the devil is a defeated foe. We cannot defeat him by our own authority; rather, he has been defeated by Jesus Christ. Jesus referred to the devil as the "ruler of this world" (John 12:31) and, Jesus said of him, "he has nothing in Me" (John 14:30). The devil has never had and will never have any authority, power, or influence over Jesus. The book of Revelation graphically details Jesus' definitive victory over the devil when He casts him "into the lake of fire and brimstone" where the devil "will be tormented day and night forever and ever" (Rev. 20:10).

You may ask, "If the devil is a defeated foe, why do we still have to fight?" The victory over the devil is assured in reality, but it is not yet accomplished in time. The fate of the devil is sealed, but he will have access to humankind until the day when God brings this age to an end. The existence of the devil is related to our having free will as human beings. God has given human beings the ability to choose, and that ability includes our right to choose evil if we so desire. The devil, as the supreme agent of evil, thus has the power to tempt us and to oppress us.

What we do know with certainty is that at *any* time the devil is confronted with Jesus, Jesus wins. When we place our faith and hope in Christ and resist the devil, the devil cannot score a definitive victory over our lives. We may lose battles against the devil from time to time, but *we will not lose the war* because we belong to Christ.

It is important to keep this assurance of victory at the forefront of our thinking as we study spiritual warfare. If we look only at the devil and his tactics, it is easy to become discouraged or fearful. If we keep our focus on Jesus Christ, however, we remain strong and alive in our spirits.

The Great Value of Christian Allies

Since everyone faces spiritual battles, every person knows what it means to come up against the devil's assaults. This is an area in our Christian walk in which each of us should have great empathy toward our brothers and sisters in Christ. One of our greatest privileges and responsibilities is to help our fellow believers fight and win spiritual battles. No person is intended to confront the devil alone. Christ assures us that He is always present. Even so, we are to function as the *body* of Christ, one to another. We are to join forces with those who are under attack by the enemy—especially those who are discouraged, depressed, or under severe oppression by the devil—and become fellow warriors, doing battle in the spirit realm through our prayers and loving support.

As you face spiritual battles, you are wise to turn to your brothers and sisters in Christ and ask for their help. As you see others facing spiritual battles, you are admonished by the Scriptures to go to them and help them win a victory through Christ Jesus. We are to fight together against our common enemy, Satan, and his demons. Imagine how much would be accomplished in our churches today if believers would band together against their true enemy, rather than waste their time and energy bickering with one another or fighting against matters of lesser importance.

Because this is a Bible study intended for group use, I encourage you to see yourselves as a band of God's warriors, powerfully equipped for battle through your relationship with Christ Jesus and your empowerment by the Holy Spirit. Expect your study of the Word to equip you to help one another as you continue to build your relationship with other believers in your church or community after your study has ended.

LESSON 1

PREPARING TO OVERCOME THE ENEMY

This book is intended for Bible study. I encourage you to refer to your Bible often as you read the lessons in this book. Mark the passages, phrases, or words that have special meaning to you. Write your insights in the margins of your Bible. In my opinion, a well-marked Bible is the genuine hallmark of a serious Bible student.

The Bible is God's foremost method of communication with us today. It is the main reference to which we must return continually to check out messages that we believe are from God. In a study of spiritual warfare, it is easy to get sidetracked into what people say about the devil or about the evil forces of darkness. We must remain in the Bible in order to avoid error or unnecessary distractions.

Keys to Study

You will be asked at various points in the lessons to identify with the material by answering one or more of these questions:

- What new insights have you gained?
- Have you had a similar experience?

- How do you feel about this?
- In what way are you challenged to act?

Insights

An insight is more than an idea or fact. It is seeing a truth from God's Word as if you are encountering it for the very first time. You may have read a verse or passage many times in the past and think that you know it well. And then, God surprises you! He reveals a new level of meaning to you in such a way that you say to yourself, "Why didn't I see that before?" That is a spiritual insight.

Insights are usually very personal—something is relevant to us because of a particular experience or situation in our lives, or something is especially meaningful in light of another passage in the Scriptures that we have been reading or studying. Every part of the Word of God is linked to every other part of the Word of God, and often these linkages are the points at which we gain spiritual insight.

Ask God to give you fresh insights every time you read His Word. I believe He'll answer that prayer.

When you have a spiritual insight, note it in your Bible. Your insight may be in the form of a question. Keep that question in mind as you continue to read God's Word. When you come to a conclusive answer, also note that in your Bible. The more we look and listen for insights, the more God gives them to us. The more we note them, the greater our understanding grows about the truths of God that run from cover to cover in the Bible.

Experiences

Each of us comes to God's Word with a unique set of personal experiences, difficulties, and accomplishments. Therefore, each person has a unique perspective on the Scripture reading. For example, the person who has been raised in church from childhood and is very familiar with Bible stories may have a different understanding of a passage from that of a person who is a new believer and is just starting to study the Bible. In a group, this difference in familiarity with the Bible can sometimes create problems. As you begin your study together, recognize that you are coming to the study with a unique background and that you can always learn something from others, even the most naive novice.

What we do have in common are life experiences. All of us can point to times in our lives when the Bible confirmed, encouraged, convicted, or comforted us in some way. We all have experiences about which we can say, "I know that truth in the Bible is real because of what happened to me."

Our experiences do not make the Bible true, of course. The Bible is absolute truth, period. Nevertheless, as we share our experiences and how they relate to the Bible, we find that God's Word applies to the human experience in more ways than we have ever thought of or personally experienced. We begin to see that the Bible speaks to each person and it addresses each emotion and general situation that a man or woman will feel or encounter in life.

Sharing experiences in your faith journey is important for your spiritual growth. Even if you are doing this study on your own, I encourage you to talk to others about your faith experiences and to be open to listening to them tell how the Bible has affected their lives.

Emotional Response

Just as we have unique backgrounds, we have unique emotional responses to God's Word. No one set of emotions is more valid than another. You may feel great relief or joy when reading a particular passage; another person may be frightened or perplexed by the same chapter of Scripture.

Face your emotions honestly. Learn to share your emotions with others. Again, your emotions do not give validity to the Scriptures. The Bible is true regardless of how you feel about it. Your faith must always be based on what God says, not on what you feel. At the same time, you are wise to recognize that the Bible has an emotional impact on you. You cannot read the Bible with an open heart and mind and not have an emotional response to it. At times you may be moved to tears, at other times you may feel great elation, longing, surprise, or hope.

Especially in a study of spiritual warfare, we have a tendency to deny our emotions regarding the devil or to adopt a stance of bravado. We can benefit greatly by identifying how we feel. This often is the starting point for our growing in faith and in courage.

In my experience with Bible study groups, I have found that it is far more valuable to share feelings than to share opinions. Scholarly commentaries have their place in teaching us the context and background of certain passages. Some people do have special insights into God's Word that are of benefit to everyone in a group setting. But, generally speaking, sharing opinions is not very productive in group study, and in some cases it can actually be counterproductive, leading to anger, mistrust, or frustration. When we share our feelings with one another, however, we become vulnerable with other people and give them the freedom to be vulnerable with us in return. This vulnerability often can open us to hearing what is truly significant for us from God's Word.

Furthermore, God often speaks to us in the language of the heart—the unspoken language of intuition, desires, and longings. When we share our feelings with one another, we grow closer to one another, and as a group, closer to the heart of God.

Challenges

In reading God's Word, we nearly always come to a point where we feel a deep stirring in our spirits, often a conviction that there is something we need to address or change in our attitudes, habits, or behavior. Sometimes this is a conviction of sin. At other times it is a clear call from God to engage in a new discipline or area of ministry.

God is never content with the status quo. He is always seeking our growth and our perfection in Christ Jesus. He prompts us from time to time as we read His Word to move forward in our Christian walk, or to move to a deeper level of faith and devotion.

When we feel God challenging us, stretching us, calling us, molding and shaping us, we are in a position to say to God, "Show me clearly what You desire for me to do." When He shows us the direction we are to take or the decisions we are to make, we must obey.

Ultimately, God desires that we read His Word and then *do* what it says. The main goal of our Bible study is to apply God's Word to our daily lives and become stronger witnesses of the love of God to every person we encounter. It isn't enough for us to clarify our insights, recall our experiences, or identify our emotions. We must live the Christian life twenty-four hours a day, seven days a week, every week of the year. We are challenged to be doers of His Word and not hearers only (James 1:22).

Studying with Others

The value of a group study is that you will be confronted with insights, experiences, and emotions that are not your own—and which will serve to stretch and challenge you. In turn, as you share your insights, experiences, and emotions, you will challenge others and also grow in your ability to communicate God's Word. There is great value in a group study experience! If you don't have someone to talk to about your insights, experiences, emotions, and challenges, I encourage you to find somebody. Perhaps you can start a Bible study in your home. Perhaps you can talk to your pastor about organizing Bible study groups in your church. Not only will you grow in your understanding of God's Word, but you will be building relationships with fellow believers that can be invaluable.

Keep the Bible Central

Keep the Bible central to your study. Don't let a Bible study group turn into a support group or a therapy group. These types of groups have their time and place, but it is as we gather around God's Word—as if we are reading the manual that will make a life-or-death difference in our lives—that we truly grow in the Lord and become all that He created and designed us to be.

If you are doing a personal Bible study, you must be diligent in maintaining your focus on God's Word. Self-analysis is not the goal of this study. Growing up in the fullness of the stature of Christ is the goal.

If you are part of a group study, make certain that your conversation about God's Word doesn't stray into a discussion of the latest news about occult practices or groups, paranormal experiences, or what a particular preacher has to say about the devil. Stay in the Word of God. Rein in all discussions so your focus is tightly on what God is saying to you through the Bible.

Prayer

I encourage you to begin your Bible study sessions in prayer. Ask God to give you spiritual eyes to see what He wants you to see and spiritual ears to hear what He wants you to hear. Ask Him to give you new insights, to recall to your memory experiences that relate to what you read, and to help you identify your emotional responses. Ask Him to reveal to you what He desires for you to be, say, and do.

As you conclude your study, ask the Lord to seal what you have learned in your heart so you will never forget it. Ask Him to transform you more into the likeness of Jesus Christ as you meditate on what you have learned. And above all, ask Him to reveal to you ways in which you can apply what you have studied and to give you the courage to live out God's Word in your daily life.

As you begin your study, consider these questions:

- *What new insights into overcoming the enemy do you hope to gain from this study?*

- *In what areas do you have questions about spiritual warfare? In what areas do you perceive a personal need for greater strength, power, or authority?*

- *How do you feel about your ability in Christ Jesus to encounter and defeat the enemy of your soul?*

- *Are you open to being challenged to engage more actively in spiritual warfare against the devil's forces?*

LESSON 2

THE NATURE OF OUR ENEMY

One of the foremost rules of warfare is: know your enemy. The more you know about your enemy—how he thinks, what motivates him, his intrinsic nature—the better you are able to devise a means of counteracting his moves and defeating him. To overcome the enemy of our eternal spirit, the devil, the first thing we must know about him is his nature.

Peter described the devil as a "roaring lion, seeking whom he may devour" (1 Peter 5:8). Most big-game hunters consider the lion the most dangerous of animals. It is extremely powerful and can move very fast and very low (out of sight in tall grassland areas). It has a great ability to track its prey, being stealthy in its maneuvers and deceptive in its motives. A lion's awesome roar instills fear that often paralyzes its prey, making conquest all the easier.

Peter accurately identified all of these characteristics with the devil. The devil is powerful, deceptive, secretive, and can act swiftly if given an opportunity to attack. His roar against us can cause us to quake in fear. Peter was writing to Christians who were enduring great persecution, and they readily understood this graphic image. The enemies of Christianity in both the Jewish and Roman communities often operated secretly, and while the early Christians knew they had enemies waiting to pounce on them for their faith, the identity of their enemies was often unknown to them.

Peter also said that the devil shows no favoritism when he attacks: "The same sufferings are experienced by your brotherhood in the world" (1 Peter 5:9). The devil acts like a roaring lion toward believers and unbelievers alike. His behavior doesn't change according to his prey; it is his *nature* to be like a roaring lion, seeking whom he may devour. A lion's actions are consistent, whether its prey is a wildebeest or a young zebra. A lion acts like a lion . . . always.

The devil is often depicted humorously as a little imp with a pitchfork sitting on a person's shoulder and whispering naughty things into a person's ear. Nothing could be farther from the truth. The devil is always seeking our destruction. He is forever on the prowl, never satisfied with his most recent kill. It is his nature to destroy, to kill, to maim, to devastate. Jesus said that the devil comes at us with the purposes of stealing anything of material value from us, killing our relationships, and destroying our physical and emotional health and ultimately, our lives (John 10:10).

The devil is a fierce opponent, a deadly enemy. There is nothing funny or humorous about his tactics or his intent, and there certainly is nothing to laugh about if you are his intended victim. We do ourselves a serious disservice if we discount his existence, take him lightly, or believe that we are capable of defeating him in our own strength.

Other Descriptions of the Enemy

Peter called the devil an "adversary" (1 Peter 5:8). An adversary is someone who opposes you. An adversary may oppose what you say or do, or he may be hostile toward you for no other reason than because you exist. A real enemy is someone who doesn't like you simply because you were born. It doesn't matter what you do or don't do—an adversary will take a stand against you. His goal is to defeat you because he wants to defeat you. He takes personal pleasure in doing so.

This means that we don't have to *do* anything to earn the devil's disapproval and hatred. Certainly, there's nothing we can do to earn the devil's approval! He is opposed even to those who give in to him and serve him. He entices and then kills his victims, often with the very thing he used to entice them. We see this all the time in our world today. People are enticed to use drugs and alcohol, and many of them die from diseases, accidents, or overdoses related to drugs and alcohol. Others turn to occult practices, only to become the victims of those same practices. Many people are drawn to crave material goods, and then pay a high penalty for stealing or embezzling the material goods of another person or a company.

Some people believe that the devil likes particular people and gives them certain powers or charms. The devil has never liked any human being. Every human being is a potential threat to him. The devil likes people about as much as a cat likes a mouse that the cat is temporarily playing with—just prior to eating it. The devil may enjoy sporting with a human being, but that should never be confused with approval or a willingness to share power or give favors.

The devil has disliked you from your birth, solely because you are a creation of God designed with a specific purpose, one that is ultimately for your good and God's glory. The devil doesn't want you to bring glory to God or to live a life that in any way points toward God's love or God's goodness. He is your *adversary*, and he will never cease to be your adversary.

The Bible has other names for the devil, all of which describe various aspects of his evil nature:

- Thief (John 10:10)
- Father of lies (John 8:44)
- Beelzebub, which refers to his being the ruler of the maggots or any agent of decay (Matt. 12:27)
- Deceiver (Rev. 12:9)
- Tempter (Matt. 4:3)
- Satan, which is a term that refers to his bringing continual accusation against those who have faith in God (Matt. 12:26)

Not one of these descriptors for the devil is flattering! There is not one ounce of good in him. He is evil to the core.

NOTE: In our study we will use the words *enemy*, *devil*, and *Satan* interchangeably.

What the Word Says	What the Word Says to Me
The thief does not come except to steal, and to kill, and to destroy. I have come that they may have life, and that they may have it more abundantly (John 10:10).	_____ _____ _____ _____ _____
He was a murderer from the beginning, and does not stand in the truth, because there is no truth in him. When he speaks a lie, he speaks from his own resources, for he is a liar and the father of it (John 8:44).	_____ _____ _____ _____ _____ _____ _____
The great dragon was cast out, that serpent of old, called the Devil and Satan, who deceives the whole world (Rev. 12:9).	_____ _____ _____ _____

- *What new insights do you have into the nature of the enemy of your soul?*

  _____

  _____

- *How do you feel about the fact that you have such an enemy?*

  _____

  _____

- *In what ways do you feel challenged to engage in efforts to overcome your enemy?*

  _____

  _____

A Satanic Attack

A satanic attack is an experience in which we sense that Satan has launched a major assault against our lives. Now, he is prowling about the edges of our lives at all times, looking for a particular point of entry. His tactic is like that of a pride of lions—to zero in on weakness, divide, and then destroy. When the devil thinks he has an opening, he attacks. We usually have a general awareness that the devil is not far away, but there are times when we are keenly aware that the devil is making a direct move against us. That is a satanic attack.

- *In your life, have you had an experience in which you sensed the devil was launching a major attack against you? How did you feel?*

_____

_____

Assurance and Warning for the Believer in Christ

If you are a believer in Christ Jesus, you should be assured that the devil cannot attack and destroy your relationship with Christ. He cannot cross the blood barrier that Christ purchased on your behalf when Jesus died on the cross at Calvary. In Christ, we have eternal life (John 3:16; 1 John 5:11–13).

Paul wrote that neither principalities nor powers could separate a person from the love of Christ (Rom. 8:38). *Principalities* and *powers* describe demonic forces. Paul also said that neither height nor depth could separate a person from Christ (Rom. 8:39). *Depth* refers in part to Sheol, the place of the dead.

What the devil can do, however, is attack you in the realm of your emotions, your mind, and your body. He moves against you so you no longer have the energy, the health, the drive, or even much of a desire to serve God. Although the devil cannot score a definitive victory over you, he can render you ineffective.

The devil also can and does attack your reputation and your witness. He always is seeking a means of destroying the testimony of a Christian, again in order to render that Christian ineffective for the gospel's sake.

The devil knows that he can't take away the eternal life of a believer. But if he is unable to destroy the believer's spirit, he'll do his best to make the believer *useless* as an advocate for God's kingdom on earth. In other words, the devil may not be able to keep you from heaven, but he will do his best to make certain you don't take anybody to heaven with you.

What the Word Says	What the Word Says to Me
Who shall separate us from the love of Christ? . . . I am persuaded that neither death nor life, nor angels nor principalities nor powers, nor things present nor things to come, nor height nor depth, nor any other created thing, shall be able to separate us from the love of God which is in Christ Jesus our Lord (Rom. 8:35, 38–39).	----------------------------------- ----------------------------------- ----------------------------------- ----------------------------------- ----------------------------------- ----------------------------------- ----------------------------------- ----------------------------------- -----------------------------------
This is the testimony: that God has given us eternal life, and this life is in His Son. He who has the Son has life; he who does not have the Son of God does not have life. These things I have written to you who believe in the name of the Son of God, that you may know that you have eternal life, and that you may continue to believe in the name of the Son of God (1 John 5:11–13).	----------------------------------- ----------------------------------- ----------------------------------- ----------------------------------- ----------------------------------- ----------------------------------- ----------------------------------- ----------------------------------- ----------------------------------- -----------------------------------

Patient and Persistent

Satan is committed to destroying you at any cost. He is patient, willing to wait for the one opportune moment of weakness that he needs to attack you. He is equally persistent; he will not give up in seeking your destruction.

We are very unwise if we think that we ever have a respite from the devil, or if we think we have conquered him once and for all in our lives, or even in one particular area of our lives. He continues to prowl, to wait, to watch, to seek a basis on which to attack us. If he can't influence us directly, he'll attempt to influence others around us in order to divert our attention from Christ or weaken our resolve to maintain the purity of our walk with Christ.

The only way to ensure that Satan does not gain an opportunity in our lives is to remain close to Christ Jesus and to seek to walk daily in the guidance and strength offered to us by the Holy Spirit. We must keep our resolve to say no to the temptation to sin, and to seek God's forgiveness quickly anytime we fail to keep God's commandments.

What the Word Says	What the Word Says to Me
He who has been born of God keeps himself, and the wicked one does not touch him (1 John 5:18).	....
I have kept away from the paths of the destroyer. Uphold my steps in Your paths, That my footsteps may not slip (Ps. 17:4–5).	....

What Satan Can and Cannot Do

As powerful and cunning as Satan may be, he is neither omnipotent nor omniscient. Nor is he omnipresent. In fact, the devil bears none of the absolute or everlasting qualities of God.

The devil was originally created by God as Lucifer, one of the archangels of heaven. As a created being, he had a beginning, and according to the book of Revelation, he will have a horrible ending—destruction and torment in a lake of fire and brimstone (Rev. 20:10).

As a creature, the devil can only be in one place at a time. Many people believe they are doing constant battle with Satan. In all likelihood, they have never had a single battle with Satan himself. The forces they have battled are Satan's demons, the fallen angels who joined Lucifer in rebelling against God. It is primarily through demons—sometimes called powers, principalities, and authorities in the Bible—that Satan exerts his influence on human beings today.

Demons have the ability to tempt. They have the ability to torment and oppress human beings, including the ability to harass Christians. Paul described demonic activity with Christians as a wrestling match (Eph. 6:11–12).

Satan himself does not indwell human beings. To do so would greatly limit his power. Demons, however, have the ability to indwell a non-Christian so that the person begins to act the same way that Satan would act if he were present on the scene.

The demons are organized and ruled by Satan. They do what he commands. The Bible tells us that the forces of darkness have a hierarchy. Paul described this to the Ephesians as "principalities ... powers ... rulers of the darkness" (Eph. 6:12).

Demonic activity is widespread and constant. In fact, John wrote, "the whole world lies under the sway of the wicked one" (1 John 5:19). The devil, the wicked one, exercises his power of influence through his demons.

While Satan and his demonic forces are powerful and prevalent, they are not sovereign. Only God is sovereign. Only God possesses ultimate authority over His universe. Satan cannot exceed the limits that God has put upon him. Neither can his demons. God may allow Satan an opportunity to tempt or to exert influence in a person's life, but God determines the extent to which He allows Satan to operate. God retains ultimate control—always.

We see this in the life of Job. Satan asked to have access to Job to torment him, and God allowed him to do so. (See Job 1:6–12; 2:1–6.) The first time Satan made his request to move against Job, the Lord said, "Behold, all that he has is in your power; only do not lay a hand on his person" (Job 1:12). Satan caused the death of Job's sons and daughters, as well as the loss of Job's herds, flocks, and servants, but Job responded by saying, "The LORD gave, and the LORD has taken away; / Blessed be the name of the LORD" (Job 1:21). He did not blame God for any of his misfortune.

The second time Satan requested of God that he be allowed to tempt Job, the Lord said, "Behold, he is in your hand, but spare his life" (Job 2:6).

In both cases, two things are important to note:

First, Satan is subservient to God. He can bring to God his accusations against a person and he can question God, but he cannot touch the person who fears God and shuns evil unless God gives him permission. (See Job 1:1.)

Second, God puts limits on what Satan is allowed to do to those who fear God and are seeking to walk before Him with a blameless and upright life. Satan cannot overstep the boundaries that God puts upon him.

At the end of Job's story, God says to Job,

> *Who then is able to stand against Me?*
> *Who has preceded Me, that I should pay him?*
> *Everything under heaven is Mine.* (Job 41:10–11)

"Everything" includes, of course, Satan and his demons. They cannot and will not succeed in their rebellion against God.

Part of the deception that Satan has played upon the minds of men and women is that he is as powerful as God, that he is an equal force to God, and that he holds just as much power for evil as God holds for good. That simply is not true. Satan operates *under* God's sovereignty. He is a rebel against a higher authority. God alone is the sovereign King of the universe and He has no equal.

What the Word Says	What the Word Says to Me
Read Job 1:1—2:10 and Job 41:10—11.	----------------------------- -----------------------------
No temptation has overtaken you except such as is common to man; but God is faithful, who will not allow you to be tempted beyond what you are able, but with the temptation will also make the way of escape, that you may be able to bear it. Therefore, my beloved, flee	----------------------------- ----------------------------- ----------------------------- ----------------------------- ----------------------------- ----------------------------- -----------------------------

from idolatry (1 Cor. 10:13–14).

"To whom then will you liken Me,
Or to whom shall I be equal?" says
the Holy One.
Lift up your eyes on high,
And see who has created
these things,
Who brings out their host by
number;
He calls them all by name,
By the greatness of His might
And the strength of His power;
Not one is missing. . . . Have you
not known?
Have you not heard?
The everlasting God, the LORD,
The Creator of the ends of
the earth,
Neither faints nor is weary.
His understanding is unsearchable
(Isa. 40:25–26, 28).

The Christian's Response: Healthy Respect, Not Cowering Fear

What then should be our response to the devil once we know his nature? I believe we should have a clear understanding of and healthy respect for the devil's power, but as Christians, we do not need to cower in fear before him. He is a defeated foe; Christ Jesus our Lord is victor over him.

The person who should truly fear the devil is the person who does not have a personal relationship with Christ Jesus—the person who has not accepted what Jesus did on the cross and who has not received God's offer of forgiveness. That person has no shield against the devil. He or she is open prey to the devil's assaults.

If you have not accepted Jesus Christ as your personal Savior and you are not seeking to walk closely with Christ today, I encourage you to own up to your sinful nature and recognize that you are living apart from God, to accept that Jesus died for your sins, to ask the Father to forgive you and transform your sin nature, and to ask God to fill you with His Holy Spirit so that you might live a life that is pleasing to Him. Unless you are a Christian, you cannot overcome the enemy of your soul. As long as you are a nonbeliever, you are one of the devil's favorite targets. You are destined to be his victim without any means of recourse as long as you remain in rebellion against God.

- *What new insights do you have into the nature of the enemy of your eternal spirit?*

  _____

  _____

- *In what ways are you being challenged today in your efforts to overcome the enemy?*

  _____

  _____

LESSON 3

THE TACTICS OF OUR ENEMY

We need to know not only the nature of the enemy of our eternal spirits, Satan, but also his tactics. A knowledge of the devil's methods better equips us both to discern the devil at work and to know better how to resist him and withstand his assaults.

Satan's primary tool is deception. He works through the processes of our minds in an attempt to get us to call good "bad" and bad "good." He is a master of twisting the truth and veiling what is harmful to us so it *appears* to be beneficial.

The devil is an expert at appearances, disguises, and false illusions. He is the master counterfeiter. The best counterfeits, of course, are objects that are most like the genuine articles. The devil specializes in "good fakes." He comes at us in a way that is appealing and appears to be very spiritual and totally acceptable. Paul referred to the devil as an "angel of light," one who is *masquerading* as one of God's holy angels.

> Satan himself transforms himself into an angel of light. Therefore it is no great thing if his ministers [demons at work in people] also transform themselves into ministers of righteousness, whose end will be according to their works. (2 Cor. 11:14–15)

Satan's best efforts are those in which a person under demonic influence *appears* to be doing something that is good, right, or noble, when, in fact, the person is operating from evil motives and for evil ends. Ultimately, the darkness in an evil person will be revealed and will destroy the person, but often not until many others are deceived and are living according to Satan's purposes.

Who are Satan's best vehicles of deception? Satan's best human agents are not the drunks sitting on a downtown street corner or the gang members who terrorize a neighborhood. Everybody knows that these people are either the victims of or the perpetuators of something that is bad. No, Satan's best agents are the brilliant, well-dressed, "successful" people who claim that they have made their way in life totally on their own intellect and skill, who refuse to acknowledge God or His Son, Jesus Christ, and who are fountains of all sorts of false philosophies. They operate in a wide variety of religions and "isms" around the world—including the religions of secularism and humanism, which worship the idols of human achievement.

These expert agents of Satan appear to be well-intentioned people who have the needs and concerns of others at heart (others nearly always being their own followers or the people they can control and manipulate). In reality, they are self-centered, godless people who are motivated by a greed for possessions and a lust for personal power.

Satan is often depicted as a bright red creature with a long pointed tail and horns growing out of his head. Believe me, if that was what Satan really looked like, nobody would be deceived by him. They would see him coming a mile away! Satan's tactics and "appearance"—which includes the way his demons work—are much more subtle. Only those who truly are discerning are able to see him at work.

The more Satan watches our lives and knows about us, the more veiled his tactics become. He rarely attacks a person head-on at their strengths. Rather, he discovers their weaknesses and bores into them over time, chipping away at their lives with persistence and increasing subtlety. It's as if the devil says, "Well, they saw through that and didn't buy my lie, so let me see if I can hide my intent a little and try another tactic that won't be so easily recognized." The more we resist the devil, the more clever and veiled are the devil's deceptions. Over time, this can reach the point where Jesus said that even those who were the strongest, most committed Christians would be in danger of becoming deceived (Matt. 24:24).

What the Word Says

False christs and false prophets will rise and show great signs and wonders to deceive, if possible, even the elect (Matt. 24:24).

That we should no longer be children, tossed to and fro and carried about with every wind of doctrine, by the trickery of men, in the cunning craftiness of deceitful plotting, but ... grow up in all things into Him who is the head—Christ (Eph. 4:14–15).

What the Word Says to Me

- *Can you recall a time when you were deceived into thinking that something bad was good? That something good was bad?*

- *Have you ever had an experience in which you were led astray by someone who seemed to be acting for good on your behalf, but who eventually was revealed as a person who was manipulating you in a way that was evil in God's eyes?*

- *What new insights do you have about your enemy?*

- *Recall a specific instance of being deceived. At what point were you aware that you were deceived? How did it feel to be deceived—both before and after the deception became apparent to you?*

The Process of Deception

Deception is a process that has several identifiable stages.

First, an idea is planted in our imaginations. Everybody has an imagination. It's a part of our thinking that we use for exploring "what if" possibilities and dreams. The imagination in and of itself is neutral. It is a mental ability that can be turned to bad or good. The person who uses his or her imagination for good can be a positive force for building up God's people and expanding the kingdom of God on earth. Such a person can envision highly innovative ways to spread the gospel and show the love of God to people who are desperately in need of His love. On the other hand, the person who allows his imagination to be used for evil can have an equally dangerous and damaging influence on others.

A key question we must ask ourselves about any new idea we have is, "Where does the implementation of this idea lead?" In other words, will implementation of the idea lead us and others to heaven, or will it lead us or others astray and cause us to be detoured away from heaven?

The first thing the devil does to deceive us is to plant an idea in our minds that has an appealing element to it. Usually our first impulse toward Satan's planted ideas is to reject them. If we do so, we can cut off Satan's efforts before we experience any negative backlash. Unfortunately, the devil's ideas always are wrapped in some element that has a certain amount of appeal to us.

He knows what we like and what we want in our fleshly desires, and he wraps up his temptation in something that appeals to us. He does this so we will at least entertain the idea a while. We may call it a "fantasy," "daydream," or "wish." We know it's wrong, but we assume that because we are only *thinking about it* there's no harm, no foul.

The more we dwell on one of Satan's ideas, the more we are trapped by it. We sometimes say that certain things or ideas "capture" our imaginations. In fact, they do! The longer an idea is entertained in the imagination, the more likely we are to act on the idea.

What the Word Says

For the weapons of our warfare are not carnal, but mighty through God to the pulling down of strongholds; casting down imaginations, and every high thing that exalteth itself against the knowledge of God, and bringing into captivity every thought to the obedience of Christ (2 Cor. 10:4–5 KJV).

Do not . . . give place to the devil (Eph. 4:26–27).

What the Word Says to Me

- *Can you recall a negative experience that began with your imagining something that was not right for you in God's eyes?*

_____

_____

- *What new insights do you have into your enemy's tactics and how to overcome him?*

_____

_____

Second, we begin to identify with the idea that the devil has planted in our imagination. We start to put ourselves into the picture. We wonder, *How would it feel to own that object . . . to be with that person . . . to go to that place . . . to participate in that activity . . . to be a part of that group?*

The longer we identify with the idea, the more we *desire* to try out the idea. We begin to dwell on the idea and it occupies more and more of our mental energy. Increasingly, we associate ourselves with what we justify to be the beneficial and appealing aspects of the idea.

In the 1960s the counterculture movement spawned the saying, "If it feels good, do it. And if you haven't tried it, don't knock it." We as a nation began to accept the idea that unless we had personal experience with something, we had no right to criticize it or call it a sin. Many people still think that way.

What has happened, however, is that Satan has taken that philosophy and couched it in even more subtle terms. Now, we justify to ourselves that it is acceptable for us to "try out an idea in our minds"—that is, to identify with it in our thoughts. We don't have any real intention of engaging in the actual experience or behavior, primarily because we don't want to be caught in the act by others who might criticize us. We justify to ourselves, however, that it just might be beneficial for us to try out a particular idea in our minds so we can see how we "feel" about a behavior or relationship. We assume that if we never actually *do* in reality what we are *doing* in our minds, we remain righteous in God's eyes.

This faulty thinking has been around for at least two thousand years, and very likely since Adam and Eve were expelled from the Garden of Eden. Jesus pointed to the danger of *identifying* with sin and responding to it in the mind and heart:

> You have heard that it was said to those of old, "You shall not murder, and whoever murders will be in danger of the judgment." But I say to you that whoever is angry with his brother without a cause shall be in danger of the judgment. . . . You have heard that it was said to those of old, "You shall not commit adultery." But I say to you that whoever looks at a woman to lust for her has already committed adultery with her in his heart. (Matt. 5:21–22, 27–28)

Jesus taught that the way we feel on the inside is just as much a reality as the way we behave on the outside. Sinning "in our minds" is just as real as sinning before the whole world. When we begin to identify with Satan's ideas, we are already in highly dangerous territory.

What the Word Says

For as he thinks in his heart, so is he (Prov. 23:7).

What the Word Says to Me

_____

_____

But Jesus, knowing their thoughts, said, "Why do you think evil in your hearts?" (Matt. 9:4).

_____

_____

_____

- *Can you recall a time in your life when you began to identify with an idea that you knew was wrong?*

_____

_____

Third, we have a growing desire to experience the full reality of Satan's sinful idea, and we begin to plot a way in which we might act out the thing we know is wrong. The more we identify with one of Satan's ideas, the stronger our desire grows to experience the idea. When that desire reaches a certain degree of intensity, our wills become involved. We begin to make a *plan* for acting out the full-blown desire that began as only a prick of our imagination.

Let me give you a couple of examples. A person might start thinking about something he knows he can't afford, perhaps a fancy new convertible sports car that costs triple the amount he has available to spend on a car. He thinks about how beautiful the car is and then about all the benefits of owning such a car. Before long, he is thinking about how good it would feel to drive the car with the top down and about how his friends would be impressed if he owned such a car. He begins to see himself sitting in it. He imagines the car in front of his house, and he fantasizes about driving it to his place of employment and parking it in his own special parking place. Before long, he is making plans to go for a test drive at a local dealership.

In another example, a woman begins to think about what it might be like to be married to a man she has met at the office. The only problem is that this man is already married. She ignores that fact and starts to think about all the benefits that might be associated with marrying this man. She begins to see herself going places with him and starts to project how envious her friends would be. Before long, she is plotting a way to get this man to have lunch with her, in hopes that she might find a way to get him to invite her out to dinner.

There's only one short step between a strong desire to experience something, own something, or take a specific action, and the making of a plan that puts that desire into action.

The Scriptures strongly advise us to check out our plans and the motives behind them.

What the Word Says	What the Word Says to Me
These . . . things the LORD hates . . . A heart that devises wicked plans (Prov. 6:16, 18).	
Let none of you plan evil in his heart Against his brother (Zech. 7:10).	
There are many plans in a man's heart, Nevertheless the LORD's counsel— that will stand (Prov. 19:21).	

- *Have you had an experience in which you desired something so much—even though you knew it was wrong—that you began to plot a way to act on your desire?*

_____

_____

Fourth, we act out the idea. In acting out an idea, we rarely have an intent of turning the action into a habit. We usually say to ourselves, "I'm just going to try this one time to see what it's like." But, generally speaking, if we try something we know to be sin, the part that was appealing to us in the first place is going to be temporarily satisfying to us, and we are going to continue to desire and do what we know to be wrong.

We try to convince ourselves that we are strong enough to say no to a second temptation, even though we haven't been strong enough to say no to the first temptation.

Once we make a decision to act out sin, we are self-deluded. We think that we can control our fleshly tendencies to sin. In reality, our fleshly tendencies, desires, and lusts are in control of us. When we give in to sin and it becomes a habit in our lives, we become addicted to our sin. It rules us. It dominates our every waking thought. It governs our every action.

Our natural human desires are strong, especially when they are coupled with our human will. Once we engage knowingly in sin, the desire for sin is even stronger and our will to sin is strengthened. We find it increasingly difficult on our own to deny ourselves what we desire. Our willpower diminishes. Only as we trust the Holy Spirit to give us the power to withstand Satan's temptations can we turn away from sin and choose God's plan for good. (See Rom. 7:15–25.)

What the Word Says	What the Word Says to Me
An oracle within my heart concerning the transgression of the wicked: There is no fear of God before his eyes.... The words of his mouth are wickedness and deceit; He has ceased to be wise and to do good. He devises wickedness on his bed; He sets himself in a way that is not good. He does not abhor evil (Ps. 36:1, 3–4).	....
The good that I will to do, I do not do; but the evil I will not to do, that I practice. Now if I do what I will not to do, it is no longer I who do it, but sin that dwells in me.... So then, with the mind I myself serve the law of God, but with the flesh the law of sin (Rom. 7:19–20, 25).	....
But I see another law in my	....

members, warring against the law of my mind and bringing me into captivity to the law of sin which is in my members. O wretched man that I am! Who will deliver me from this body of death? I thank God—through Jesus Christ our Lord! (Rom. 7:23–25).

- *Have you had an experience in which you told yourself you were only going to try something "once," only to find yourself trying that same thing repeatedly?*

_____

_____

- *What new insights do you have into the tactics of your enemy and how to overcome him?*

_____

_____

All Sin Begins with Satan's Ideas

All of us are thinking constantly. Both the Holy Spirit of God and Satan have access to our minds. We do not "think thoughts" totally on our own initiative. Our minds, our imaginations, are the soil in which the Holy Spirit plants seed ideas that will bear a harvest of blessing in our lives. In like manner, Satan has been allowed to *attempt* to plant seeds that have no other potential than to become wild weeds of destruction.

We must choose to let the thoughts that are from God remain and take root in us. With great diligence, we must choose to let the thoughts that are from Satan fly right on by. We must refuse to entertain Satan's notions or to engage in fanciful imaginations about evil.

Peter gave us great wisdom about how we can avoid the devil's process of deception: "Be sober, be vigilant" (1 Peter 5:8).

Sober. To be sober means to have a clear mind. We are not to have any fuzzy thinking about what is right and what is wrong. We are to know with certainty the commandments of God and the teachings of Jesus so we will know instantly if an idea is from Satan or from the Holy Spirit. It is our responsibility to maintain a sober mind. No one else can read and study God's Word for us. We must do it ourselves. We must set our minds to learn what is right and what is wrong from God's perspective.

To be sober also implies a seriousness about life. We are not to joke about the devil or take him lightly. We are to recognize that we have an enemy who wants only one thing—to wipe us out. If he can't wipe us out, he'll settle for the next best thing—to render us ineffective and useless. We must take our enemy as seriously as he takes us.

Vigilant. To be vigilant means to be watchful, to be alert, to always be quick to say no to the devil. How do we stay vigilant? We ask the Holy Spirit to help us stay vigilant! The devil has never pulled the wool over the eyes of the Holy Spirit. The devil has never deceived the Holy Spirit, whom Jesus described as being the Spirit of truth. Our vigilance is directly related to our reliance upon the Holy Spirit to guide us in our daily decisions and choices. If we ask the Holy Spirit with a sincere heart to reveal to us the lies of the devil and to discern evil spirits at work, we can be assured that He will do so.

God has never asked us to overcome the enemy on our own strength. He gives us the Holy Spirit to help us overcome the enemy. We, however, must choose to receive the Holy Spirit's help. Being sober and being vigilant mean being serious about following God in every area of our lives, twenty-four hours a day, every day.

- *In what ways do you feel challenged in your walk with the Lord?*

_____

_____

LESSON 4

A POSTURE OF ACTIVE RESISTANCE

The term *resistance movement* is frequently used to describe conflict situations where oppressed people rise up against their oppressors. Those who are part of resistance movements take the stance, "I'm not going to stand idly by and allow this evil to continue. I choose to resist the wrongs that have been and are being perpetuated against me and those I love. Whether I live or die in resisting my oppressor, I will no longer live as I have been living."

A seldom-recognized fact about resistance movements is this: they succeed. If people genuinely have been oppressed and the resistance movement has identified and targeted the true oppressors, the resistance movement nearly always achieves its goals. The oppressors are overthrown. That is not to say that new oppressors might not arise. What it does say is that when enough people say no to evil with a loud enough voice for a long enough period of time, evil is overcome. Those who are evil lose power, retreat, or withdraw when faced with sufficient resistance.

Throughout history, we have many examples of people who resisted evil in ways that were not militant, vengeful, or violent. In fact, most of the Christian martyrs through the ages were people who took a stand against evil, resisting all attempts to get them to deny the Lord

Jesus, turn their back on their faith, or expose their fellow Christians to harm. Their resistance made a difference, and in the end Christ has proved victor. Christ's kingdom on earth expands; the human-made kingdoms of oppressors fade into history.

Resistance is the biblical approach to confronting and overcoming the devil. Peter wrote, "Resist him, steadfast in the faith" (1 Peter 5:9). James echoed this teaching: "Submit to God. Resist the devil and he will flee from you. Draw near to God and He will draw near to you" (James 4:7–8). Both Peter and James make clear that we are to actively resist evil.

Active Resistance

On the surface, resistance may appear to be passive. In practice, it is anything but passive. It is an active stance that is intentional and powerful.

Think for a moment about what you would do if you saw a large person running directly toward you at a rapid pace. Imagine that there is a sheer wall to your right and a sharp drop-off to your left. There's no way you can turn and outrun this apparent adversary who is coming at you like a bowling ball headed straight for the only pin left in the lane. What do you do? You very likely brace yourself for the hit. You plant your feet squarely and lean forward, probably with one shoulder and leg a little ahead of your other leg and shoulder. You grit your teeth, tense your muscles, and prepare for the blow, fully expecting that your adversary will bounce off you rather than knock you down. You are in a position of resistance.

Think for a moment about what you would do if a weight began to press against you in an attempt to push you off a position that you knew was rightfully yours to occupy. How would you resist? You would lean into the weight and press back. The pressure you would exert would be as much as the pressure being exerted against you. That's a posture of resistance.

Resistance is when we row against the tide of the culture and refuse to adopt evil practices just because the majority of people around us appear to be adopting them.

Resistance is when we do the right thing, solely because it is the right thing to do.

Resistance is refusing to go along with those who invite us to participate in activities that bring no glory to God and are contrary to His commandments.

Resistance is saying no to offers of drugs and other harmful substances.

Resistance is holding the line for a good cause.

Resistance is first and foremost a firm decision to engage in the struggle against evil, rather than turning away, backing off, or retreating from the devil's attack.

- *Can you recall an experience when you were required to engage in active resistance?*

_____

_____

- *How do you feel about the Bible's admonition to resist the devil?*

_____

_____

Resistance and Patience

Resistance takes strength and courage. It also takes patience.

> Be patient, brethren, until the coming of the Lord. See how the farmer waits for the precious fruit of the earth, waiting patiently for it until it receives the early and latter rain. You also be patient. Establish your hearts. (James 5:7–8)

Not only are we to be patient with ourselves, but we are to be patient with our fellow believers. We must look with hope to the future that the Lord has for each one of us. The good work that He is doing in us, He is doing in others around us—perhaps in different ways and at a different pace. If we become impatient with our spiritual growth or that of others, it is easy to become angry, frustrated, and unloving. Such attitudes give an opportunity for Satan to work. They are not attitudes of resistance. Resistance is patient.

What the Word Says	What the Word Says to Me
Do not grumble against one another, brethren, lest you be condemned. . . . My brethren, take the prophets, who spoke in the name of the Lord, as an example of suffering and patience. Indeed we count them blessed who endure. You have heard of the perseverance of Job and seen the end intended by the Lord—that the Lord is very compassionate and merciful (James 5:9–11).	------------------------------- ------------------------------- ------------------------------- ------------------------------- ------------------------------- ------------------------------- ------------------------------- ------------------------------- ------------------------------- -------------------------------
Love suffers long and is kind . . . bears all things, believes all things, hopes all things, endures all things (1 Cor. 13:4, 7).	------------------------------- ------------------------------- ------------------------------- -------------------------------

- *What new insights do you have into overcoming your enemy?*

_____

_____

How to Resist

Peter and James point to two key words that are at the heart of our ability to resist the devil: *submission* to God and *faith*.

Submission. Submission to God is saying, "I can't. You can." In our resistance against the devil, we might say, "I can't defeat the devil on my own. But with You, I can." Certainly this is the position the apostle Paul took when he said, "I can do all things through Christ who strengthens me" (Phil. 4:13).

James described submission in part as occurring when we seek to develop a closer relationship to God: "Draw near to God and He will draw near to you" (James 4:8).

How do we draw near to God? The number one way to get to know God and to know *how* He wants us to overcome evil and experience blessing is to spend time with God. It's virtually impossible to have a close relationship with someone if you have no communication! We draw near to God in prayer and in time spent reading God's Word. We draw near to God when we set aside time solely to listen to God and to wait upon Him for direction and guidance. We draw near to God when we periodically shut ourselves away with God, closing off all other influences that might distract us from knowing Him better.

The closer we draw to God, the better we know Him. And the better we know Him, the more we see His awesome power, experience His vast love, learn from His wisdom, and grow in our faith. We come to an even greater realization and conclusion: "Yes, God *can* defeat the devil on my behalf. Yes, God *will* win in any conflict with the devil. Yes, God *does* want me to be able to overcome my adversary and to live in victory in Christ Jesus."

Those who submit their lives to God are humble. Humility and submission cannot be separated. The truly humble are those who recognize that they are totally dependent upon God, and that only God is God. The person who believes the truth about God with all of his or her heart receives an abundant portion of God's grace (James 4:6).

- *Have you totally surrendered your life to Christ? Have you completely submitted your will and desires to God?*

  _____

  _____

- *How does total surrender and submission feel? If you have not surrendered or submitted your entire life to Christ, how do you feel when you hear the words* surrender *and* submit?

  _____

  _____

Faith. Faith is saying to God, "I believe You will." In our battle to overcome the enemy, our faith might be stated this way: "I believe You will defeat the enemy and cause him to flee from me as I resist him and put my trust in You." Again and again, David made this declaration of faith to the Lord: "O my God, I trust in You." (See Pss. 25:2; 31:6; 55:23; 56:3; 143:8.)

Each of us has been given a measure of faith from our birth (Rom. 12:3), but this does not mean that we automatically have an active, vibrant, or mature faith. Our faith can lie dormant in us, for the most part unused. It also can remain a weak or immature faith. Jesus referred to "great faith" and "little faith" (Matt. 6:30; 8:10, 26). The disciples asked specifically that Jesus increase their faith (Luke 17:5). The implication is clearly that our faith is capable of growth.

Our faith becomes alive and active when we recognize who we are in Christ. "Christ in me" is one of the most powerful statements of faith a person can make, for Christ has far greater power than any force of the devil. (See 1 John 4:4.)

How do we grow in faith? By using our faith. By trusting God in situation after situation, circumstance after circumstance, relationship after relationship. We develop a personal history in which we have been faithful in our obedience to God and He has been faithful in His loving care of us.

Much of what is said about faith in God's Word is couched in terms of our walking in faith or standing in faith. *Faith is to be applied.* It is to be exercised and developed. When we stand in faith, we are saying, "I am fully persuaded that God is God and I cannot be moved from that position." When we walk in faith, we are saying, "I have every confidence that God is with me wherever I am, and that He will remain with me forever. I am fully convinced that He is working all things together for my eternal and highest good." (See Rom. 8:28.)

Remaining steadfast in our faith—staying grounded, keeping our resolve, refusing to give in to doubt or fear—is an act of our will. We must *choose* to remain steadfast in faith. The Holy Spirit will help us in this if we ask for His help. He is the One who gives us the power to endure the assault of the enemy against us, even to the last moment of our lives.

- *In what ways are you being challenged in your spirit regarding your faith?*

_____

_____

The Bible has much to say about both submission and faith. As you read through the selected verses below, relate them to the concept of resistance.

What the Word Says	What the Word Says to Me

Submitted to God:

Humble yourselves in the sight of the Lord, and He will lift you up (James 4:10).

I beseech you therefore, brethren, by the mercies of God, that you present your bodies a living sacrifice, holy, acceptable to God, which is your reasonable service (Rom. 12:1).

Then the people rejoiced, for they had offered willingly, because with a loyal heart they had offered willingly to the LORD (1 Chron. 29:9).

Do not be stiff-necked, as your fathers were, but yield yourselves to the LORD; and enter His sanctuary, which He has sanctified forever, and serve the LORD your God (2 Chron. 30:8).

Then the priest said, "Let us draw near to God here." So Saul asked counsel of God (1 Sam. 14:36–37).

It is good for me to draw near to God;
I have put my trust in the Lord GOD,
That I may declare all Your works (Ps. 73:28).

Therefore, brethren, having

boldness to enter the Holiest by
the blood of Jesus . . . let us draw
near with a true heart in full assurance of faith, having our hearts
sprinkled from an evil conscience
and our bodies washed with pure
water. Let us hold fast the confes-
sion of our hope without wavering,
for He who promised is faithful
(Heb. 10:19, 22–23).

God resists the proud,
But gives grace to the humble
(James 4:6).

Steadfast in Faith:

He who is in you is greater than he
who is in the world (1 John 4:4).

Pursue righteousness, godliness,
faith, love, patience, gentleness.
Fight the good fight of faith, lay
hold on eternal life (1 Tim.
6:11–12).

Jesus answered and said to them,
"Assuredly, I say to you, if you have
faith and do not doubt . . . whatever things you ask in prayer,
believing, you will receive" (Matt.
21:21–22).

As you therefore have received
Christ Jesus the Lord, so walk in
Him, rooted and built up in Him
and established in the faith, as you
have been taught, abounding in it
with thanksgiving (Col. 2:6–7).

And you, who once were alienated
and enemies in your mind by

wicked works, yet now He has reconciled in the body of His flesh through death, to present you holy, and blameless, and above reproach in His sight—if indeed you continue in the faith, grounded and steadfast, and are not moved away from the hope of the gospel which you heard (Col. 1:21–23).

Hold fast the pattern of sound words which you have heard from me, in faith and love which are in Christ Jesus. That good thing which was committed to you, keep by the Holy Spirit who dwells in us (2 Tim. 1:13–14).

Therefore, my beloved brethren, be steadfast, immovable, always abounding in the work of the Lord (1 Cor. 15:58).

- *What new insights do you have into the importance of submission to your ability to overcome the devil?*

  _____

  _____

- *What new insights do you have into the importance of your faith in overcoming the devil?*

  _____

  _____

Faith, Submission, and Resistance Are Connected

In the battle against our adversary, our faith in Christ Jesus, our submission to God, and our resistance against the enemy are closely connected.

You can resist the devil only if your faith is strong. It is impossible for you to resist the devil for very long if you do not believe that Christ Jesus in you can and *will* defeat the devil.

Furthermore, you can be firm in your faith only if you are completely submissive to God. That means you submit all areas of your life. When you do not submit an area to God you are saying to God, in effect, "I can handle this. I don't need Your help." That's precisely the place the devil will attack you!

The good news is that God has given each of us a measure of faith to develop. We are capable of submitting. And therefore, we are capable of resisting the devil.

When we do, he must flee.

- *Recall an experience in which you resisted the devil and he did flee. To what degree were humble submission and steadfast faith involved?*

_____

_____

- *In what ways are you being challenged in your spirit?*

_____

_____

LESSON 5

DEVELOPING A DISCERNING SPIRIT

Many of God's people are in trouble today because they do not have a discerning spirit. They walk right into Satan's traps and never even know what happened to them. One of them might say, "I can't imagine what went wrong." A person with a discerning spirit will be quick to explain, "Here's the trap Satan set and here's how you fell into it."

Each of us needs to develop a discerning spirit and to teach our children how to have a discerning spirit. A discerning spirit is rooted in a knowledge of right and wrong. The time to begin teaching discernment, and to teach right and wrong to our children, is not when they reach adulthood. We teach it to them from the time they are very young children.

Moses told the Israelites they must thoroughly train their children in God's commandments:

> These words which I command you today shall be in your heart. You shall teach them diligently to your children, and shall talk of them when you sit in your house, when you walk by the way, when you lie down, and when you rise up. You shall bind them as a sign on your hand, and they shall be as frontlets between your eyes. You shall write them on the doorposts of your house and on your gates. (Deut. 6:6–9)

We must know right from wrong not only in theory, but in practice. We must know how to *apply* God's truth to our lives and how to live in obedience to His commandments. That's why Moses said that we are to teach our children God's commandments throughout the day, not just in a half-hour Sunday school lesson. We are to say plainly to them, "This is right behavior, this is wrong behavior. This is God's commandment. This is the consequence for breaking God's commandment. "An education in right and wrong must occur twenty-four hours a day, every day of the year.

A child who is thoroughly trained in God's commandments and has been taught right from wrong has very little trouble discerning Satan at work. He quickly picks up signals that tell him when things are not right; his conscience is sensitive.

A child who is not taught right from wrong—a child who is allowed to do whatever he wants to do without consequence and is told that all things are relative and that there are no absolutes—becomes a slow-moving target for the enemy. He never sees what hits him.

There have been times when I've entered a room full of people and immediately sensed in my spirit that something was not right. It's as if an inner alarm had gone off. At times the room was even occupied by a group of Christians—but my inner spiritual radar told me that something was amiss, something wasn't right before God. In every case, I've discovered that this inner discernment was correct.

I believe each Christian can and should be developing and exercising this kind of spiritual discernment. God does not want His people to live in darkness or to be without an ability to detect evil at work. He has made every provision necessary for us to acquire and grow in our ability to discern our enemy.

God's provision for us is twofold: His Word, and His Spirit. The Bible is our sourcebook for right and wrong. God's Spirit is our teacher in helping us to choose good in our daily walk with Christ.

What the Word Says	What the Word Says to Me
A wise man's heart discerns both time and judgment, Because for every matter there is a	

time and judgment (Eccl. 8:5–6).

And they shall teach My people the difference between the holy and the unholy, and cause them to discern between the unclean and the clean. In controversy they shall stand as judges, and judge it according to My judgments. They shall keep My laws and My statutes (Ezek. 44:23–24).

For everyone who partakes only of milk is unskilled in the word of righteousness, for he is a babe. But solid food belongs to those who are of full age, that is, those who by reason of use have their senses exercised to discern both good and evil (Heb. 5:13–14).

• *How are you being challenged in your spirit?*

_____

_____

The Critical Importance of Knowing God's Principles

You will maintain or grow in your knowledge of right and wrong only by remaining steadfastly in God's Word. If your parents did not teach you right from wrong at an early age, it is imperative that you retrain your mind. You can do this by reading God's Word on a consistent, daily basis.

Believe what you read. Accept God's Word at face value. God means what He says. He says what He means.

Apply what you read. Put God's Word to use. Do what it says to do.

God's Word will renew your mind as you read it, giving you increasing insight into what God considers to be righteous and unrighteous behavior, activities, and attitudes. In fact, I believe as you read God's Word on a daily basis over time, your desires will change. You will no longer feel drawn to or comfortable in certain settings or situations. You will develop a deep intuitive understanding that you simply do not belong in certain relationships or groups.

Even if you had a wonderful Christ-centered childhood in which you gained a strong sense of right and wrong, you benefit greatly by staying in God's Word on a daily basis. What you have learned in the past is reinforced in your mind and heart. So much in our culture today presents an upside-down version of the truth—right is called wrong (or rigid, insensitive, extremist, or narrow-minded), and wrongdoing is called right (especially "in certain situations" and "given certain circumstances"). Blame is placed on everything except the exercise of free will that God gave each of us to make personal choices. A steady and consistent reading of God's commandments helps to keep us from falling victim to false teachings and human philosophies.

What the Word Says	What the Word Says to Me
Be diligent to present yourself approved to God, a worker who does not need to be ashamed, rightly dividing the word of truth (2 Tim. 2:15).	------------------------------ ------------------------------ ------------------------------ ------------------------------ ------------------------------
All Scripture is given by inspiration of God, and is profitable for doctrine, for reproof, for correction, for instruction in righteousness, that the man of God may be complete, thoroughly equipped for every good work (2 Tim. 3:16–17).	------------------------------ ------------------------------ ------------------------------ ------------------------------ ------------------------------ ------------------------------ ------------------------------
Guard what was committed to your trust, avoiding the profane and idle babblings and contradictions of what is falsely called knowledge—by professing it some	------------------------------ ------------------------------ ------------------------------ ------------------------------ ------------------------------

have strayed concerning the faith
(1 Tim. 6:20–21).And do not be
conformed to this world, but be
transformed by the renewing of
your mind, that you may prove
what is that good and acceptable
and perfect will of God (Rom.
12:2).

The Simplicity of the Truth

Don't try to complicate or read your own meanings into God's Word. God has not made His Word too difficult for you to comprehend. You may benefit from a translation of the Scriptures that presents God's truth in more modern English so you can better understand the language of the Bible. But the *truths* of the Bible are actually quite plain. We are the ones who make the Bible complicated in our attempts to justify our own desire to sin or to "explain away" the passages that we find difficult to obey.

Paul warned the Corinthians that "as the serpent deceived Eve by his craftiness, so your minds may be corrupted from the simplicity that is in Christ" (2 Cor. 11:3).

What happened in the Garden of Eden? Satan came to Eve and asked, "Has God indeed said . . . ?" He planted a doubt in her mind. He implied that Eve may not have accurately heard God or that she had come to a wrong conclusion about what God meant. Eve began to read into God's commandment more than God had said. She replied, "God has said, 'You shall not eat it, nor shall you touch it, lest you die'" (Gen. 3:3). That's not precisely what God had commanded Adam. He had told Adam, "Of the tree of the knowledge of good and evil you shall not eat." Eve added something to God's Word.

Next, Satan tried to get Eve to believe that it would be good for her to eat the fruit of the tree because it would make her more like God. If she was more like God she wouldn't die, because God will never die. Satan complicated the message. He introduced confusion and questioning. If Eve had stayed obedient to God's plain and simple commandment she would have been fine. The commandment was straightforward and easy to understand. The same is true for virtually all of God's commandments.

If you do not understand parts of God's Word, ask God to reveal to you what you need to know in order to live your life in a way that is pleasing to Him. The fact is, you may not need to have a full understanding of the depth of every verse in the Bible. Some of the information in the Bible is likely to be understood fully only after we are with the Lord in heaven. But, we can be assured that God will reveal to us everything we need to know in order to live godly lives each day we are on earth. We can trust the Holy Spirit to teach us and remind us of the truth we need as we face specific situations, decisions, and choices.

What the Word Says	What the Word Says to Me
The Helper, the Holy Spirit, whom the Father will send in My name, He will teach you all things, and bring to your remembrance all things that I said to you (John 14:26).	------------------------------ ------------------------------ ------------------------------ ------------------------------ ------------------------------ ------------------------------
If any of you lacks wisdom, let him ask of God, who gives to all liberally and without reproach, and it will be given to him (James 1:5).	------------------------------ ------------------------------ ------------------------------ ------------------------------
Ask, and it will be given to you; seek, and you will find; knock, and it will be opened to you. For everyone who asks receives, and he who seeks finds, and to him who knocks it will be opened (Matt. 7:7–8).	------------------------------ ------------------------------ ------------------------------ ------------------------------ ------------------------------

Getting Rid of the Clutter

Much of what we take into our minds is of no eternal use to us. It has virtually no benefit in helping us live our daily lives. It serves as clutter and it results in confusion. Not only do we need to turn to God's Word on a daily basis, but we need to turn *away* from the messages and sources of information that present an image of the world that is contrary to God's desire.

We must refuse to listen to *false teachers*—those who often appear to be Christians but in fact do very little to lead a person to Jesus or to help a person walk in close relationship with the Holy Spirit. We must also refuse to listen to *teachers of falsehood*—those who present messages to us that are impure, violent, rooted in greed, or which present human beings as the center of the universe.

What the Word Says	What the Word Says to Me
Remain in Ephesus that you may charge some that they teach no other doctrine, nor give heed to fables and endless genealogies, which cause disputes rather than godly edification which is in faith. Now the purpose of the commandment is love from a pure heart, from a good conscience, and from sincere faith, from which some, having strayed, have turned aside to idle talk, desiring to be teachers of the law, understanding neither what they say nor the things which they affirm (1 Tim. 1:3–7).	-----------
Now the Spirit expressly says that in latter times some will depart from the faith, giving heed to deceiving spirits and doctrines of demons, speaking lies in hypocrisy, having their own conscience seared with a hot iron (1 Tim. 4:1–2).	-----------
Reject profane and old wives' fables, and exercise yourself toward godliness (1 Tim. 4:7).	-----------

- *What new insights do you have into the importance of discernment and how to acquire it?*

  _____

  _____

- *In what ways are you being challenged in your spirit?*

  _____

  _____

Staying Sensitive to Your Surroundings

Many Christian people have crashed in their spiritual lives because they had no spiritual sensitivity to what was happening around them. We must ask the Holy Spirit to help us remain alert and aware of the opportunities, challenges, and temptations that come our way.

Throughout the Scriptures we find the admonition to "watch." We are to watch so we can guard against enemy attack. We are also to watch for what the Lord desires to bring our way; we are to remain sensitive always to the blessings and opportunities that the Lord desires to give us. We must watch for ways in which God wants to use us to bring blessings to others.

In ancient times, watchmen were assigned to stand on the walls of fortified cities. They worked in shifts that provided round-the-clock coverage. Their responsibility was twofold: watch for the approach of enemies who were intent on attack, and watch for the appearance of the king's emissaries or the king himself. Our role as discerning Christians today is the same: we are to watch alertly and consistently for the Lord's appearance in our midst as much as we remain alert to the possibility of enemy attack.

This means we must be continually alert for ways in which to share the gospel with others who do not know Jesus as their Savior. We must be aware of what God is desiring to do in us and through us as ambassadors for Christ on earth. We must be on constant alert for opportunities to do good and to give words of loving encouragement to our fellow Christians.

Ask the Holy Spirit to help you "watch." I believe He will move quickly to answer that prayer.

What the Word Says	What the Word Says to Me
Watch and pray, lest you enter into temptation. The spirit indeed is willing, but the flesh is weak (Matt. 26:41).	------------------------------- ------------------------------- -------------------------------
Be serious and watchful in your prayers (1 Peter 4:7).	------------------------------- -------------------------------
But concerning the times and the seasons, brethren, you have no need that I should write to you. . . . For when they say, "Peace and safety!" then sudden destruction comes upon them, as labor pains upon a pregnant woman. And they shall not escape. But you, brethren, are not in darkness, so that this Day should overtake you as a thief. You are all sons of light and sons of the day. We are not of the night nor of darkness. Therefore let us not sleep, as others do, but let us watch and be sober (1 Thess. 5:1, 3–6).	------------------------------- ------------------------------- ------------------------------- ------------------------------- ------------------------------- ------------------------------- ------------------------------- ------------------------------- ------------------------------- ------------------------------- ------------------------------- ------------------------------- ------------------------------- ------------------------------- ------------------------------- ------------------------------- ------------------------------- -------------------------------
Blessed is he who watches (Rev. 16:15).	------------------------------- ------------------------------- -------------------------------

- *Can you recall a time when you experienced a negative consequence primarily because you were not sensitive to your surroundings or to what the Lord was desiring to do in a particular situation?*

- *In what ways are you being challenged in your spirit?*

_____

_____

Remain in Complete Submission to God

The flip side of submission is *reliance*. When you are submitted to someone, you are at the same time reliant on that person. For example, when you yield or submit your personal defensive power to another person, you become reliant on that other person to protect and shield you. When you submit your ability to provide for yourself to another person, you become reliant on that other person to meet your needs. When you submit to the decision-making authority of a person above you, you become reliant on that person to exercise wisdom and justice on your behalf.

This is a very important concept related to spiritual discernment. With our finite mental ability, we simply cannot discern clearly all of the tactics and influences of the devil. The devil is not omnipotent, but he is more powerful than any human being. The devil is not omniscient, but he knows more than any human being. The devil is not omnipresent, but he's been around a lot longer than any human being on earth today. The result is that the devil has cunning tricks that are beyond our abilities as human beings to perceive or understand.

In order to exercise sound spiritual discernment, you must submit to God's authority and become reliant on God's discerning power to work in you. Your submission to God includes your submission to the authority of His Word, the Bible. God expects you to do what He tells you to do. As you obey His commandments, He takes on the responsibility for all of the consequences related to your obedience. When you trust God's Word to be true, it is then up to God to be faithful to His Word and to perform what He has said He would do on your behalf.

Your submission to God also includes submission to the authority of the Holy Spirit over your life. As a Christian, you are not abandoned to survive on your own in an evil world. But neither are you given free reign to do whatever you want to do. You are in a line of authority under God the Father, and the Holy Spirit is your immediate supervisor. Submission to and reliance on the Holy Spirit must be ongoing in your life; it is a daily submission, not a one-time event.

How does this relate specifically to discernment?

Your prayer and mine must be, "Holy Spirit, I submit myself to You. I want to do only what You want me to do. I want to shun evil and pursue good. I am trusting You to reveal to me any sin in my life, any error that I am about to make. I am putting myself into a position to be totally reliant on You to show me which choice to make, which path to pursue, which opportunity to seize, which relationship to forge, which call to answer. I am also totally reliant on You to reveal to me the presence of evil or an attack of the devil on my life, and to show me how I might resist the devil and overcome him. Help me."

What the Word Says	What the Word Says to Me
Blessed is the man who makes the LORD his trust, And does not respect the proud, nor such as turn aside to lies (Ps. 40:4).	------------------------------- ------------------------------- ------------------------------- ------------------------------- -------------------------------
I am poor and needy; Make haste to me, O God! You are my help and my deliverer; O LORD, do not delay (Ps. 70:5).	------------------------------- ------------------------------- ------------------------------- -------------------------------
My eyes are upon You, O GOD the Lord; In You I take refuge; Do not leave my soul destitute. Keep me from the snares they have laid for me, And from the traps of the workers of iniquity. Let the wicked fall into their own nets, While I escape safely (Ps. 141:8–10).	------------------------------- ------------------------------- ------------------------------- ------------------------------- ------------------------------- ------------------------------- ------------------------------- ------------------------------- ------------------------------- ------------------------------- -------------------------------

Discernment Develops as We Stay Focused on God

Our ability to discern develops as we

- stay in the Word on a daily basis.
- stay sensitive to what is happening around us and to those we encounter who may be in need.
- stay submitted to God's commandments and to the daily direction of the Holy Spirit.

Our focus must be tightly on God and His plans, purposes, and principles. When we are walking closely with the Holy Spirit, discernment comes naturally and quickly.

Discernment is critical if we are to sidestep the traps that the devil has set for us. In fact, discernment is the key to our avoiding many of life's troubles and trials.

- *What new insights do you have into discernment and its relationship to overcoming the devil?*

  _____

  _____

- *In what ways are you being challenged in your spirit?*

  _____

  _____

LESSON 6

ENGAGING IN WARFARE

No rank-and-file member of the military engages in warfare on his own initiative. Specific military orders must come from those who have the authority to wage war. Even the president of the United States, the commander in chief of the military, cannot declare outright war without an act of Congress.

In the body of Christ, we are under the authority of our spiritual commander in chief, Jesus Christ our Lord. He is the One who authorizes us to engage in warfare against the devil.

This is an important concept to understand. We *do* have the authority to fight the devil. That authority has been given to each of us by Jesus. At the same time, if Jesus had not given us authority to wage war with our adversary, we would have no basis on which to fight him and no chance of overcoming him.

Our battle orders against Satan come from Jesus and from Him alone. He is our commander in the battle. He is the One who fights on our behalf and wins the victory.

Matthew 12 records Jesus' response to the Pharisees when they accused Him of casting out demons by the power of Beelzebub, the ruler of the demons. Jesus' statement conveys an important message to us today as we battle our adversary:

> Every kingdom divided against itself is brought to desolation, and every city or house divided against itself will not stand. If Satan casts out Satan, he is divided against himself.

How then will his kingdom stand? And if I cast out demons by Beelzebub, by whom do your sons cast them out? Therefore they shall be your judges. But if I cast out demons by the Spirit of God, surely the kingdom of God has come upon you. Or how can one enter a strong man's house and plunder his goods, unless he first binds the strong man? And then he will plunder his house. He who is not with Me is against Me, and he who does not gather with Me scatters abroad. (vv. 25–30)

In other words, Jesus told the Pharisees:

- If Satan casts out Satan, he is divided against himself.
- Every kingdom divided against itself will not stand.
- If a person is not with Me in battling demonic power, He is against Me.

Although Jesus was addressing the Pharisees, what He said is significant to us. If we are not 100 percent *with* Jesus in battling our adversary—if we are relying on any other source of power apart from that of the Holy Spirit of God—then we are actually against Jesus and our efforts at defeating Satan will fail.

We cannot defeat the devil with our intellect.

We cannot defeat the devil with our clever reasoning.

We cannot defeat the devil with our hatred of him.

We can defeat the devil only by relying totally and completely on Jesus Christ to work in us and through us and on our behalf. There is no successful warfare against the devil apart from Him. He authorizes our war against the devil, even as He empowers us to win it and gives us the courage to engage in it.

- *What new insight do you have into your authority to engage in spiritual warfare?*

_____

_____

Assurance of Victory

When we engage in warfare at Christ's command and under His authority, we are assured of victory. When it feels as if we're losing the battle, there are two key points to keep in mind:

1. *The loss of a battle is not the loss of the war.* In some cases, you may feel as if you have lost a round in your fight against the devil. You may experience what you perceive to be a setback. When Jesus sent out His disciples to preach the gospel and heal the sick, He said that if the people in a city did not receive them, they were to wipe the dust of that place from their feet, give a warning to the people, and move on. Jesus anticipated that His disciples might not be successful 100 percent of the time.

Nevertheless, Jesus expected His disciples to continue to move forward, doing the maximum amount of good and preaching and praying with the greatest amount of effectiveness possible in any given town, village, or rural area. He expects the same of us. He does not call us to be successful, but rather, faithful. We are to do what He calls us to do; the consequences and results are His responsibility.

2. *The final victory will be revealed fully in eternity.* You do not know the full impact that you have on the lives of others. Some of what you accomplish for Christ on earth will be revealed to you only in eternity. And when it comes to eternity, the devil has absolutely no hold on you once you have accepted Christ as your Savior and Lord. Nothing that the devil can do to you will change your eternal destiny.

When Jesus sent out seventy of His disciples, two by two, He gave them specific instructions to preach the gospel and heal the sick, which included anything that might keep a person from being whole. The disciples returned to Jesus with great joy, saying, "Lord, even the demons are subject to us in Your name" (Luke 10:17). Jesus responded,

> I saw Satan fall like lightning from heaven. Behold, I give you the authority to trample on serpents and scorpions, and over all the power of the enemy, and nothing shall by any means hurt you. (Luke 10:18–19)

Throughout the Scriptures, *serpents* and *scorpions* are other terms for demons. Jesus told His disciples then, and He tells us today, that His followers have authority over the devil, and the devil can do nothing to cause eternal harm to those who call on the authority of Christ. We may get scared and feel pain from time to time, but we will not experience any eternal damage.

- *What new insights do you have into your ability to engage success-fully in spiritual warfare?*

_____

_____

- *In what ways are you feeling challenged in your spirit?*

_____

_____

What Does Jesus Authorize Us to Do?

The question then naturally arises: What does Jesus authorize us to do in battling our adversary?

First, Jesus expects us to enter Satan's domain with boldness, but only after we have "bound the strong man," which is the demonic entity that has a hold on a person.

When confronting the Pharisees about the source of His own spiritual authority and power, Jesus referred to the power it takes to enter a strong man's house (Matt. 12:29). Jesus laid claim to having all the power necessary to walk into the devil's domain, pick up those whom the devil had maimed or oppressed, and bring them out of the devil's prison so they might be completely delivered and made whole. He could do this because He was able first to bind the devil.

If we are to enter the devil's domain, we also must first bind the strong man who holds power over a person. That person, of course, may be our own self. How do we do this? By keeping God's commandments, speaking God's words, and doing God's works.

The verses below relate to the importance of keeping God's statutes, and doing and saying what God tells us to do and say. As you read them, ask yourself, "How does my *doing* what these verses say to do bind the devil and render him ineffective?"

Keep in mind, also, that there are all types of bondage. Some people are bound today by habits that they can't seem to break. Some are bound in prejudices that others have taught them from their birth. Still others are bound in poverty or ignorance. Some are bound in relationships with people who are committed to evil.

The Word of God and the love of God's people putting that Word into action are sufficient for breaking *all* types of bondage. There isn't a form of bondage that cannot be broken by the Lord, if we will only say and do what the Lord requires of us.

What the Word Says	What the Word Says to Me
Judge not, and you shall not be judged. Condemn not, and you shall not be condemned. Forgive, and you will be forgiven (Luke 6:37).	----------------------- ----------------------- ----------------------- ----------------------- -----------------------
Just as you want men to do to you, you also do to them likewise. . . . Love your enemies, do good, and lend, hoping for nothing in return; and your reward will be great, and you will be sons of the Most High (Luke 6:31, 35).	----------------------- ----------------------- ----------------------- ----------------------- ----------------------- ----------------------- ----------------------- -----------------------
If you forgive the sins of any, they are forgiven them; if you retain the sins of any, they are retained (John 20:23).	----------------------- ----------------------- ----------------------- -----------------------
Go therefore and make disciples of all the nations, baptizing them in the name of the Father and of the Son and of the Holy Spirit, teaching them to observe all things that I have commanded you (Matt. 28:19–20).	----------------------- ----------------------- ----------------------- ----------------------- ----------------------- -----------------------

Watch, stand fast in the faith, be
brave, be strong. Let all that you
do be done with love (1 Cor.
16:13–14).

Jesus also said this, "Whatever you bind on earth will be bound in heaven, and whatever you loose on earth will be loosed in heaven" (Matt. 18:18).

We bind the forces of evil by praying against them and resisting them. As we discussed in a previous lesson, we resist by submitting ourselves completely to God and standing firm in our faith. If we are walking in close friendship with Christ Jesus, we render the forces of evil ineffective. We have them bottled up, tied up, locked up. They have no toehold against us. They are "bound" in their efforts to tempt us or harm our eternal spirits.

We loose the force of God's saving love and grace on the earth by giving our witness for Christ Jesus, both in word and in deed, by loving others, and by forgiving those who have sinned against us.

- *Can you recall an experience in which you were involved in the binding of the devil's attempts to bring eternal harm to a person?*

_____

_____

Second, we are to limit the access that Satan has to our lives.

In addressing the Pharisees, Jesus spoke of entering a strong man's house. This concept of "entering" is not limited to our moving into the devil's domain. The broader principle that Jesus taught includes this truth: we must not allow the devil entrance into our own house where he might cause us harm.

You, as a believer in Christ, have authority over what you will allow to enter your life. You have the power to control your thoughts. You have the power to determine what you will put into your body and how you will relate to people. You have the power to develop your own faith and to instill good spiritual disciplines into your life. You have the power to choose or change your habits, perspectives, and attitudes.

- *Can you recall a negative experience in your life that likely resulted because you did not guard the entrance to your life?*

_____

_____

Third, Jesus is present in the binding process of our adversary. Indeed, He is the One who does the binding.

Jesus said to Peter and His disciples:

> On this rock I will build My church, and the gates of Hades shall not prevail against it. And I will give you the keys of the kingdom of heaven, and whatever you bind on earth will be bound in heaven, and whatever you loose on earth will be loosed in heaven. (Matt. 16:18–19)

The rock to which Jesus referred was Peter's great statement of faith about Jesus: "You are the Christ, the Son of the living God" (Matt. 16:16). That is the central truth to our faith. The church that truly believes that Jesus is the Christ, the Son of the living God, is a church against which the "gates of Hades" cannot win. In the time of Jesus, the gates of a city were the place of government and authority. All key decisions regarding a city were made by those who sat in the city gates. Jesus was saying that the power of the devil, the demonic authorities of hell itself, cannot win against a Christ-focused church. The church, of course, is comprised of all who have accepted Jesus as their Savior and are following Him as their Lord. We are a part of the greater church and this message of Christ is for us—hell cannot win against us.

Jesus said that He gives the "keys of the kingdom of heaven" to those who are in His church. When you hold the keys to a place, you determine who goes into it. You control the access. Again, the devil cannot enter into an area of your life unless you give him access to that area.

Finally, Jesus assures us that what we do to bind the devil's power on earth is accomplished and sealed definitely and eternally in heaven. And anything Jesus does has eternal consequences!

- *In what ways are you being challenged in your spirit?*

_____

_____

You Aren't Expected to Fight a War by Yourself

Jesus taught that there is great power in agreement. An individual is not to engage in spiritual warfare on his or her own. None of us are called to be an army of one. We are to live and work and give witness and engage in warfare against our enemy as the *body* of Christ.

Jesus said;

> If two of you agree on earth concerning anything that they ask, it will be done for them by My Father in heaven. For where two or three are gathered together in My name, I am there in the midst of them. (Matt. 18:19–20)

Some spiritual battles you face may be intensely personal. Nevertheless, I encourage you to find at least one other person who can be a prayer partner with you as you resist the devil and pray for God's will to be accomplished in your life or the life of someone you love. You are likely to find that you are able to engage in your battle with greater courage and bring the battle to a successful end much more quickly if you ask for the prayers of others. God does not intend for us to live our spiritual lives in isolation.

What the Word Says	What the Word Says to Me
Confess your trespasses to one another, and pray for one another, that you may be healed (James 5:16).	_____ _____ _____
Brethren, pray for us (1 Thess. 5:25).	_____ _____
Read Acts 4:1–31.	_____

Now, Lord, look on their threats,
and grant to Your servants that
with all boldness they may speak
Your word, by stretching out Your
hand to heal, and that signs and
wonders may be done through the
name of Your holy Servant Jesus
(Acts 4:29–30).

- *How do you feel when you are in a spiritual battle by yourself? How do you feel when you are in warfare with others by your side?*

Our Spiritual Armor

Paul described to the church at Ephesus our warfare against the devil:

> Be strong in the Lord and in the power of His might. Put on the whole armor of God, that you may be able to stand against the wiles of the devil. For we do not wrestle against flesh and blood, but against principalities, against powers, against the rulers of the darkness of this age, against spiritual hosts of wickedness in the heavenly places. Therefore take up the whole armor of God, that you may be able to withstand in the evil day, and having done all, to stand. Stand therefore, having girded your waist with truth, having put on the breast-plate of righteousness, and having shod your feet with the preparation of the gospel of peace; above all, taking the shield of faith with which you will be able to quench all the fiery darts of the wicked one. And take the helmet of salvation, and the sword of the Spirit, which is the word of God; praying always with all prayer and supplication in the Spirit, being watchful to this end with all perseverance and supplication for all the saints. (Eph. 6:10–18)

I want you to notice four key things about this passage of Scripture: *First, our warfare is spiritual.* We must never become confused and think that our warfare is against a particular person or group of people. The evil that exists in our world today has its origins in the spiritual realm, and we are to go directly to the source of the evil and do our fighting there.

Second, the armor that we put on is Christ. Every piece of armor that Paul described is directly related to Jesus. We are to put on the truth of Jesus, the righteousness of Jesus, the gospel of peace embodied in Jesus, faith in Jesus as God's Son, and the salvation that Jesus purchased for us. We are to pick up the Word of God—upon which Jesus based all His words—as if it is our sword.

Every facet of our defense against our adversary is acquired when we "put on Christ Jesus."

What the Word Says	What the Word Says to Me
Put on the Lord Jesus Christ, and make no provision for the flesh (Rom. 13:14).	------------------------------------- ------------------------------------- -------------------------------------
For you are all sons of God through faith in Christ Jesus. For as many of you as were baptized into Christ have put on Christ (Gal. 3:26–27).	------------------------------------- ------------------------------------- ------------------------------------- -------------------------------------

How do we put on Christ? With our faith. What we believe about Christ, we must actively receive into our lives. We then must speak and act as if we have what we believe we have! We say to the Lord:

- "I believe You are the way, the truth, and the life and that if I follow the leading of Your Holy Spirit, You will never lead me astray. I trust You to show me what to do in the situation I am facing right now."
- "I believe Your righteousness is imparted to me through the Holy Spirit and that as I obey Your commandments, You will manifest Your character traits in me."
- "I believe that the path You have for me to walk is one that is for my good, for my wholeness, and that I will experience Your peace as I walk in it."

- "I believe that Jesus is God's only begotten Son and that He died on the cross for me and for the forgiveness of my sins. I believe You will preserve and protect my spirit so that I might have eternal life with You in heaven."

Third, our posture in warfare is primarily one of resistance. Only one piece of the armor Paul describes has an offensive use. Every other aspect is for our defense, so we might "withstand in the evil day," "quench the fiery darts of the wicked one," and be able to "stand."

Fourth, once we have put on Christ we are to pray. Where do we stand? We stand in the presence of God Himself. We come to Him in prayer.

Before we take any other action, we are to pray. Prayer is the first and foremost thing we must do anytime we feel we are under attack by the enemy or that God is calling us to engage in spiritual warfare over a particular need or situation.

We are to pray with perseverance—with enduring power—until God's supernatural power is released in us and through us. We are to be "watchful" in our prayers, alert and diligent. In the next lesson we will cover what we are wise to say in our prayers.

By putting on Christ, standing, and praying, we will be "strong in the Lord and in the power of His might" (Eph. 6:10). When we are strong in Christ, we cannot be defeated!

- *What new insights do you have into your role in spiritual warfare?*

  _____

  _____

- *In what ways are you feeling challenged in your spirit?*

  _____

  _____

THREE THINGS THE ENEMY HATES TO HEAR

Have you ever avoided a certain person solely because you didn't like what that person had to say? Perhaps the person used profane or filthy language that offended you. Or perhaps the person always made negative comments. Some people who are not Christians dislike being around people who are because they don't like hearing them talk about Jesus, God's love, the work of the church, or the ministry of the Holy Spirit.

Just as each of us is uncomfortable around certain people because of what they talk about, so the devil is uncomfortable around Christians who talk about things the devil hates. Three things the devil specifically hates to hear are:

1. The name of Jesus
2. The references to the shed blood of Jesus on the cross
3. The quoted Word of God

In our prayers against the devil, we are wise to emphasize the things that the devil doesn't want to hear!

The Power of the Name of Jesus Christ

On their way to the temple one day, Peter and John encountered a lame man who was asking for alms. This man had been lame from birth, and daily he was carried to the beautiful gate to beg for money. Peter and John fixed their eyes on the man, and Peter said to him, "Look at us." When the man had given them his attention, Peter said, "Silver and gold I do not have, but what I do have I give you: In the name of Jesus Christ of Nazareth, rise up and walk" (Acts 3:6). The Scriptures tell us that Peter then took the man by his right hand and lifted him up, and as he did, the lame man's feet and ankle bones received strength. Although he had never walked in his life, he was able to stand, walk, and leap about, all the while praising God.

Peter and John were doing what Jesus had told them to do. Jesus had said to His disciples on the night before His crucifixion, "Most assuredly, I say to you, whatever you ask the Father in My name He will give you. Until now you have asked nothing in My name. Ask, and you will receive, that your joy may be full" (John 16:23–24).

The name of Jesus is not something that we simply tack onto our prayers, however. Jesus gave to His disciples, including us, the "power of attorney" to use His name. When we pray "in the name of Jesus," we are praying as if Jesus Himself is praying. We are to pray what He would pray, asking for what He would request of our heavenly Father. A prayer that is truly in the name of Jesus is totally in line with God's Word and God's will.

The name of Jesus embodies all of the power and majesty that are rightfully Jesus' alone. His name is higher than any other name that can be named. His power is greater than that of any person or any demon. (See Phil. 2:9–11.)

The name of Jesus is a constant reminder to the devil that he is not as great or as powerful as Jesus. He does not have the relationship with the Father that Jesus has, nor is he the one who is the rightful heir to all of heaven. The devil doesn't want to be reminded of those truths.

What the Word Says

[I] do not cease to give thanks for you, making mention of you in my prayers . . . that you may know what is the hope of His calling, what are the riches of the glory of His inheritance in the saints, and what is the exceeding greatness of His power toward us who believe . . . far above all principality and power and might and dominion, and every name that is named, not only in this age but also in that which is to come. And He put all things under his feet, and gave Him to be head over all things to the church (Eph. 1:16, 18–22).

Now it happened, as we went to prayer, that a certain slave girl possessed with a spirit of divination met us, who brought her masters much profit by fortune-telling. This girl followed Paul and us, and cried out, saying, "These men are the servants of the Most High God, who proclaim to us the way of salvation." And this she did for many days. But Paul, greatly annoyed, turned and said to the spirit, "I command you in the name of Jesus Christ to come out of her." And he came out that very hour (Acts 16:16–18).

Therefore God also has highly exalted Him and given Him the name which is above every name, that at the name of Jesus every

What the Word Says to Me

----

knee should bow, of those in
heaven, and of those on earth, and
of those under the earth, and that
every tongue should confess that
Jesus Christ is Lord, to the glory of
God the Father (Phil. 2:9–11).

- *What new insights do you have into the use of the name of Jesus in overcoming the enemy?*

The Power of the Shed Blood of Christ

When we pray, we enter into the throne room of God solely on the basis that Jesus Christ died for our sins so that we might be restored to a right relationship with our heavenly Father. Throughout Scripture, we find evidence of the shedding of blood as the means God provided for His children to be reconciled both to Himself and to one another.

After Adam and Eve sinned in the Garden of Eden, God shed the blood of animals and made coats of animal skins for Adam and Eve to wear. These coats were a consistent reminder to them that God alone is the Giver, Author, and Ruler of all life. (See Gen. 3:21.)

When the time came for the children of Israel to leave Egypt and go to the Land of Promise, God required them to put the shed blood of lambs on the doorposts of their homes. When the death angel passed over the nation, it did not touch the firstborn that lived in homes where the blood had been applied. Again, God was making a provision for *life* through the shedding of blood. (See Ex. 12:12–13.)

In giving the Law, God required that animals be sacrificed. The shedding of blood was the means of reconciliation between God and people. (See Lev. 14:12–13.)

The shed blood of Jesus on the cross was God's definitive act in providing forgiveness for all who would receive it. Jesus' death was the one substantive and final sacrifice for atonement. By His shed blood, Jesus purchased humankind's forgiveness from sin.

Jesus said His death was for the "new covenant" and that His blood was "shed for many for the remission of sins" (Matt. 26:28).

In dying for our sins, Jesus dealt a mortal blow to the devil. That was His victory moment over Satan. No longer would Satan have access to Him to tempt Him. No longer would Satan have opportunity to keep Him from fulfilling God's purposes. Satan became a defeated foe the moment Jesus died on the cross.

In the shed blood of Jesus, we have the means for forgiveness and eternal life. We also have protection against our adversary, who ultimately is the agent of all that results in destruction and death. When we engage in spiritual warfare against the devil, we are wise to pray, "By the authority of Jesus Christ and under the protection of His shed blood, I pray against you, Satan."

The blood of Jesus is a terrible reminder to Satan that he lost his battle with Jesus, and that he has no power over anything that Jesus purchased with the price of His own blood.

What the Word Says	What the Word Says to Me
You were not redeemed with corruptible things, like silver or gold, from your aimless conduct received by tradition from your fathers, but with the precious blood of Christ, as of a lamb without blemish and without spot (1 Peter 1:18–19).	....
The blood of Jesus Christ His Son cleanses us from all sin (1 John 1:7).	....
You are worthy . . . For You were slain, And have redeemed us to God by Your blood Out of every tribe and tongue and people and nation, And have made us kings and	....

priests to our God;
And we shall reign on the earth
(Rev. 5:9–10).

- *What new insights do you have into the power of the blood of Jesus Christ to defeat the devil?*

_____

_____

The Power of the Quoted Word of God

The third thing that the devil cannot stand to hear is the quoted Word of God. When we quote Scripture to the devil, we need to be very specific, just as Jesus was when He was tempted by Satan in the wilderness.

> Now when the tempter came to Him, he said, "If You are the Son of God, command that these stones become bread." But He answered and said, "It is written, 'Man shall not live by bread alone, but by every word that proceeds from the mouth of God.'" Then the devil took Him up into the holy city, set Him on the pinnacle of the temple, and said to Him, "If You are the Son of God, throw Yourself down. For it is written: 'He shall give His angels charge over you,' and, 'In their hands they shall bear you up, / Lest you dash your foot against a stone.'" Jesus said to him, "It is written again, 'You shall not tempt the Lord your God.'" Again, the devil took Him up on an exceedingly high mountain, and showed Him all the kingdoms of the world and their glory. And he said to Him, "All these things I will give You if You will fall down and worship me." Then Jesus said to him, "Away with you, Satan! For it is written, 'You shall worship the Lord your God, and Him only you shall serve.'" Then the devil left him, and behold, angels came and ministered to Him. (Matt. 4:3–11)

Each time the devil tempted Jesus, Jesus responded with the Word of God. He didn't rely on human opinion or a quote from a so-called expert. Nor did Jesus command the devil to do anything other than to depart from Him. Jesus quoted Scripture, and the power of the Scripture was sufficient in defeating Satan. If that method was good enough for Jesus to use, it should be good enough for you and me.

Note, too, that Jesus used Scriptures that related directly to each of Satan's temptations. Jesus was very precise in His use of the Scriptures. For a person to be that precise in the use of Scripture, he or she must know the Bible. The person must be familiar with the truths of the Bible from cover to cover.

Think of your Bible as being filled with a full set of statements that operate as live ammunition. The verses of the Bible are powerful weapons to use as you command the devil to depart from you. The Word of God indeed is your "sword" against your adversary (Eph. 6:17).

In quoting the Scriptures to the enemy, find a passage of the Bible that is directly related to the problem you are facing. Read that passage of Scripture aloud as part of your prayers, voicing your belief in God to act for good on your behalf.

What the Word Says	What the Word Says to Me
The word of God is living and powerful, and sharper than any two-edged sword, piercing even to the division of soul and spirit, and of joints and marrow, and is a discerner of the thoughts and intents of the heart (Heb. 4:12).	
Direct my steps by Your word, And let no iniquity have dominion over me (Ps. 119:133).	
"He who has My word, let him speak My word faithfully. What is the chaff to the wheat?" says the LORD. "Is not My word like a fire?" says the LORD,	

"And like a hammer that breaks
the rock in pieces?" (Jer.
23:28–29).

- *What insight do you have into the power of God's Word in overcoming the enemy?*

Speaking to the Devil with Purity of Heart

When you speak the name of Jesus to the devil, talk to the devil about the blood of Jesus, or quote the Word of God to the devil, you must do so with a pure heart that is totally reliant on and submitted to the Lord Jesus Christ. The name of Jesus is not a magic word. The blood of Jesus is not a secret formula. We must never use the name of Jesus or make a reference to His blood in a cavalier or joking manner. Our battle with the enemy is deadly serious. Our position in Christ is the most important aspect of our lives. As Peter said, "Be sober, be vigilant" (1 Peter 5:8).

- *How do you feel about the weapons that God has given you to use in prayer?*

- *In what ways are you being challenged in your spirit?*

LESSON 8

SAYING NO TO SATAN'S WORLD ORDER

In recent years, people have spoken about our having a new world order. They generally have been referring to the realignment of political power in the aftermath of the Soviet Union's collapse.

The Bible speaks of a world order. The term *new*, however, is never applied to it. It is as old as humanity. In 1 John 2:15–17 we have a description of this world order:

> Do not love the world or the things in the world. If anyone loves the world, the love of the Father is not in him. For all that is in the world—the lust of the flesh, the lust of the eyes, and the pride of life—is not of the Father but is of the world. And the world is passing away, and the lust of it; but he who does the will of God abides forever.

A strong and related statement is found in 1 John 5:19:

> We know that we are of God, and the whole world lies under the sway of the wicked one.

The world order depicted in the Bible is not one in which Christians are to be involved. It is a world order established by our adversary. While it is not eternal, it is pervasive on the earth today. We must resist and counteract it virtually every day of our lives.

The good news is that we can! John holds out this hope:

> For whatever is born of God overcomes the world. And this is the victory that has overcome the world—our faith. Who is he who overcomes the world, but he who believes that Jesus is the Son of God? (1 John 5:4–5)

Through Christ, we have the wisdom and strength to live in a way that is opposed to Satan's world order.

What Comprises the "World"?

The Bible uses the word *world* in three ways. First, it refers to the inhabited world, the sum of the nations. Jesus said, "Go into all the world and preach the gospel to every creature" (Mark 16:15). He was sending His disciples into all the inhabited regions and nations of the world.

Second, *world* is used to describe the whole of humanity. Jesus said, "For God so loved the world that He gave His only begotten Son, that whoever believes in Him should not perish but have everlasting life" (John 3:16). Jesus was referring to all the people of the earth.

Third, *world* is used to refer to a world system, or a world order. In Ephesians 2:1–2, Paul wrote, "And you He made alive, who were dead in trespasses and sins, in which you once walked according to the course of this world, according to the prince of the power of the air, the spirit who now works in the sons of disobedience." Paul was referring to the way the cosmos operates.

Although Paul perhaps gives us the best definition of the world, the word *world* is used 185 times in the New Testament, 105 of which occur in the writings of John. John spent most of his ministry life in cities located on what is now the west coast of Turkey, cities that at the time were heavily Greek in culture and Roman in rule. John was aware that the way in which Jesus lived and ministered was 180-

degrees opposed to the normal systems and ways of Greek and Roman cultures.

Cosmos. The word *cosmos* refers literally to an arrangement of things. It is the key concept in understanding the devil's world order. The devil has a design, an "arrangement" that he desires to perpetuate upon humanity.

Every facet of life has an arrangement: politics, education, art, commerce, science, music, law. Each of these areas works in a particular way and functions under certain laws. The overall way in which these facets of life work together and function to create a culture is an even larger arrangement, a cosmos. The fact that things are arranged and ordered is not what is wrong. It is the *way* in which things are arranged and the mind that does the arranging that are the concern.

The Perfect World Order. The perfect world order is found in the first two chapters of Genesis. Adam and Eve were given the responsibility for governing a perfect world in a perfect way. In this perfect cosmos, God was in charge and Adam and Eve were completely reliant upon Him. They made only wise decisions because they trusted God to tell them what to do and how to do it. They enjoyed a perfect relationship, one without manipulation, corruption, or sin, because their relationship mirrored perfectly the relationship they had with God.

The Current World Order. The perfect world order established by God in the Garden of Eden collapsed when Adam and Eve sinned. In the wake of their fall into sin, another world order was established. This world order included the influence of Satan and his ability to manipulate and control humanity. In this world order, Satan sought to be the ruler of the earth, the one on whom humankind is reliant and the one to whom humankind turns for all decisions.

Every variety of world order since the demise of the Garden of Eden has been structured on the same premise: Satan is seeking to be in absolute and total charge of all humankind. He desires to be the sovereign world ruler.

Of course the natural laws of the earth, such as gravity, were established by God and cannot be violated without consequences that

God also established. The unchanging laws of God include spiritual laws and laws related to the mind and emotions of humankind. The *systems of this world*, however—the organized power structures and the way they work—are largely under Satan's domain. As John said, "the whole world lies under the sway of the wicked one" (1 John 5:19).

- *In your experience, what "systems of the world" do you have to deal with on a routine basis?*

_____

_____

While God allows Satan's influence on the earth, He also has placed a limitation on him. Jesus clearly stated that limitation:

> Now is the judgment of this world; now the ruler of this world will be cast out. And I, if I am lifted up from the earth, will draw all peoples to Myself. (John 12:31–32)

Jesus was speaking of His ministry to heal the sick and deliver the demon-possessed and demon-oppressed, as well as His crucifixion on the cross. He was saying that those who believed in Him and accepted His sacrificial death on the cross as their means of forgiveness and reconciliation with God would no longer be in the grip of Satan. They would be free to live in total obedience to and reliance upon God. They, therefore, need not live as victims of Satan's world order. They would still live *in* the world, but their behavior and attitudes would not be *of* the world (John 17:14–16).

What the Word Says	What the Word Says to Me
Jesus answered, "My kingdom is not of this world . . . My kingdom is not from here." Pilate therefore said to Him, "Are You a king then?" Jesus answered, "You say rightly that I am a king. For this cause I was born, and for this cause I have come into the world, that I should bear witness to the truth.	------------------------------ ------------------------------ ------------------------------ ------------------------------ ------------------------------ ------------------------------ ------------------------------ ------------------------------

Everyone who is of the truth hears My voice"(John 18:36–37).

[Jesus said], "I have given them Your word; and the world has hated them because they are not of the world, just as I am not of the world. I do not pray that You should take them out of the world, but that You should keep them from the evil one. They are not of the world, just as I am not of the world" (John 17:14–16).

- *What new insights do you have into Satan's operation of a world order?*

_____

_____

Satan's Ploys

Satan uses two main ploys to draw men to himself so they might live according to his design.

First, he makes his world order as attractive as possible. Satan does everything he can to make his world order highly appealing. The fact, however, is that attractiveness fades. Nothing that is held out by Satan as being attractive can remain attractive. That's because everything Satan controls is seeded with Satan's own decay.

Second, he makes promises he cannot keep. Every one of Satan's temptations is a "promise" of something that will be pleasurable, beneficial, and worthy of our participation. That promise is always short-lived. It cannot be fulfilled or maintained because it is not grounded in God's eternal goodness.

We must recognize Satan's purpose behind his ploys. Satan seeks our destruction, our demise, our death. His tricks are just that, tricks. He does not desire for us to flourish, prosper, or be blessed. All that he offers is an *illusion* of goodness. The realities of his world order are deceit, confusion, pain, suffering, and despair.

We also must recognize that Satan is supremely self-centered. Everything that he does is designed to magnify his self-serving power and his self-seeking glory. He isn't the least bit interested in sharing what he has amassed with anyone else. He is only interested in duping people to give him what they have, including their souls. In the end, everything that Satan holds out to humankind as being wonderful ends up being terrible.

- *Have you ever been a victim of Satan's ploys? How did you feel at the time? How did you feel when you realized that what Satan had promised or held out as attractive was false?*

_____

_____

Satan's Lies

Satan's world order is governed by three principal lies.

First, Satan says man can be self-sufficient. Satan's foremost lie to humankind appeals directly to people's greatest fear, loss of control, and people's biggest character flaw, pride. Satan's lie is, "You don't need God. You can make it on your own." This is the lie that he voiced to Eve in the Garden of Eden. He said, "In the day you eat of it your eyes will be opened, and you will be like God, knowing good and evil" (Gen. 3:5).

God says, "You need a Source for your life. You are limited in power, wisdom, and ability. I am your Source. Furthermore, because you have been birthed with a sin nature, you need a Savior. I have provided Jesus Christ to be your Savior."

What the Word Says	What the Word Says to Me
The wicked in his proud countenance does not seek God; God is in none of his thoughts (Ps. 10:4).	_____ _____ _____ _____

Pride and arrogance and the
evil way
And the perverse mouth I hate.
Counsel is mine, and sound
wisdom;
I am understanding, I have
strength.
By me kings reign,
And rulers decree justice.
By me princes rule, and nobles,
All the judges of the earth.
I love those who love me,
And those who seek me diligently
will find me (Prov. 8:13–17).

Now we have received, not the
spirit of the world, but the Spirit
who is from God, that we might
know the things that have been
freely given to us by God (1 Cor.
2:12).

- *Recall an incident in which you were the victim of a person who had believed the lie that people can be self-sufficient.*

- *What insights do you have into the devil's manipulation of humans through a lie of self-sufficiency?*

Second, Satan says the pursuit of pleasure is man's purpose on the earth. Satan's lie is that if it feels good, looks good, or says it is good ... acquire it, possess it, or participate in it. From Satan's standpoint, there are no illegitimate desires and all of man's lusts should be fulfilled.

God says that our desires must be filled in righteous ways or we will suffer severe consequences.

What the Word Says

What the Word Says to Me

Adulterers and adulteresses! Do you not know that friendship with the world is enmity with God? Whoever therefore wants to be a friend of the world makes himself an enemy of God (James 4:4).

Pure and undefiled religion before God and the Father is this: . . . to keep oneself unspotted from the world (James 1:27).

What comes out of a man, that defiles a man. For from within, out of the heart of men, proceed evil thoughts, adulteries, fornications, murders, thefts, covetousness, wickedness, deceit, lewdness, an evil eye, blasphemy, pride, foolishness. All these evil things come from within and defile a man (Mark 7:20–23).

Do not let sin reign in your mortal body, that you should obey it in its lusts. And do not present your members as instruments of unrighteousness to sin, but present yourselves to God as being alive from the dead, and your members as instruments of righteousness to God (Romans 6:12–13).

• *Recall an incident in which you were the victim of a person who had believed the lie that people should pursue happiness at all costs.*

_____

_____

- *What insights do you have into the devil's manipulation of people through the lie that the pursuit of happiness is the reason for existence?*

_____

_____

Third, Satan says that security exists in possessions. Satan's lie is that people can purchase adequate defense, social status, and self-esteem. *Things* are exalted by Satan, as opposed to relationships.

God's truth is that only God is our true defender, provider, and shield against evil. Only God gives us a genuine feeling of self-worth. We come to this sense of our worthiness when we realize that God sent His only Son to die in order that we might live. Any status that we have, we have solely because God allows us to hold that position for purposes of effecting and expanding His kingdom.

What the Word Says	What the Word Says to Me
For what will it profit a man if he gains the whole world, and loses his own soul? Or what will a man give in exchange for his soul? (Mark 8:36–37).	_____ _____ _____ _____ _____
Do not lay up for yourselves treasures on earth, where moth and rust destroy and where thieves break in and steal; but lay up for yourselves treasures in heaven, where neither moth nor rust destroys and where thieves do not break in and steal. For where your treasure is, there your heart will be also (Matt. 6:19–21).	_____ _____ _____ _____ _____ _____ _____ _____ _____ _____ _____

- *Recall an incident in which you were the victim of a person who had believed the lie that people can acquire status or self-esteem through possessions.*

_____

_____

- *What insights do you have into the devil's manipulation of man through the lie that possessions give self-worth and security?*

_____

_____

Priority on "Self" and "Now"

You'll note that each of Satan's lies places top priority on self, and on the present. Satan does not want you or anybody else to have a concern for other people, or a concern for how your actions today might affect the future. Certainly we can look at our world today and see that people are primarily concerned with self, not God. Today's generation lives for today.

The three main lies of Satan are expressed by John as

1. *the pride of life*—humankind is completely self-sufficient.
2. *the lust of the flesh*—humankind's happiness and the fulfillment of all fleshly desires are supreme.
3. *the lust of the eyes*—humankind's position and security can be acquired by the acquisition of what man sees. (1 John 2:16)

- *What new insights do you have into the way Satan's world order is based upon lies?*

_____

_____

How to Live Free of Satan's World Order

Jesus offers us hope and assurance that humankind can be free of Satan's lies and live in truth. Truth is the key to staying out of the treachery of Satan's world order.

The truth of God is that God's commandments give us the most fruitful, beneficial, and blessed way to live. We live in truth and avoid

Satan's world order when we seek to know God's statutes and live according to them.

The truth of God is that Jesus Christ purchased our freedom from Satan through His death on the cross, and we can live in that freedom every day of our lives. We live in truth and avoid Satan's world order when we accept Jesus as our Savior and rely on Him daily to deliver us from evil.

The truth of God is that we do not need to be like this world. We can be transformed into the image of Christ Jesus. We live in truth and avoid Satan's world order when we ask the Holy Spirit to change our habits and our attitudes, and to make us more and more like Jesus.

What the Word Says	What the Word Says to Me
Then Jesus said, . . . "If you abide in My word, you are My disciples indeed. And you shall know the truth, and the truth shall make you free" (John 8:31–32).	-------------------------------
Stand fast therefore in the liberty by which Christ has made us free, and do not be entangled again with a yoke of bondage (Gal. 5:1).	-------------------------------
Do not be conformed to this world, but be transformed by the renewing of your mind, that you may prove what is that good and acceptable and perfect will of God (Rom. 12:2).	-------------------------------

Our Responsibility to Live Godly Lives

Our responsibility as Christians is not to live a life that has the world's approval. The Scriptures tell us we are to live godly lives, regardless of the cost:

The grace of God that brings salvation has appeared to all men, teaching us that, denying ungodliness and worldly lusts, we should live soberly, righteously, and godly in the present age. (Titus 2:11–12)

As Christians, we will never have the approval of the world and we waste our time if we try to win it. Rather than seek the approval of the world, we need to recognize that we are to be a light to the world, a bright witness to the truth of God's love and saving grace.

Refuse to compromise with the world order that has been established by Satan. Refuse to participate in it. You are called to be a citizen of God's heavenly kingdom, which is an out-of-this-world, eternal, perfect order.

- *What new insights do you have into how to overcome the enemy?*

_____

_____

- *In what ways are you being challenged in your spirit?*

_____

_____

FACING THE SPIRIT OF ANTICHRIST

Throughout history, greedy men have risen to power to promote their own personal causes. They nearly always couch themselves as the answer to a particular problem or even as the savior of the world. In all cases to date, by the time these people reached a certain level of prominence and power, godly people had searched the Scriptures and concluded that they were not the Christ.

In some cases, the same godly people concluded that the leader in question was the Antichrist. To date, they have all been wrong. We have not yet experienced the presence of the Antichrist, for when he makes his appearance, the entire world will know his identity because he will loudly proclaim it.

A Person or A Spirit?

Is the Antichrist a person or a spirit? The answer is both. There will be a person whose doctrine and deeds will earn him the title of Antichrist. There also is a prevailing spirit of antichrist at work in our world today.

The Person Called Antichrist

The Antichrist will be a real man who will assume a right to world rulership and be the very embodiment of evil. He will be filled with and directed by Satan himself. In the book of Revelation, John refers to this man as the Beast. He will manifest supernatural powers and exert global influence. (See Rev. 13.)

The Spirit of Antichrist

The word *antichrist* appears only in the epistles of John. John's concern was far more with the *spirit* of antichrist, whom he regarded as Satan himself, than with the person who would one day be filled with Satan and dominate the world stage. John saw Christians as being in a real and present struggle with the devil, who seeks to be a false christ—a substitute, an "instead of" christ.

The prefix *anti* has two meanings. The first conveys the idea of *being in place of something*. The second conveys the idea of *being opposed to something*. Satan always seeks to be in place of Christ; he is always opposed to Christ. He is *anti*-Christ in everything he says and does. He is the ultimate representation of ideas and behaviors opposed to Jesus.

Many people have operated in the spirit of antichrist. This type of spirit is not a demon. Rather it is a philosophy, a mind-set, a way of thinking and behaving.

The Bible refers to several types of spirit. We each have a human spirit. Romans 8:16 tells us, "The Spirit Himself bears witness with our spirit that we are children of God." There is a spirit of the world as a whole, which is the prevailing philosophy of the world order we discussed in the last lesson. Paul wrote, "Now we have received, not the spirit of the world, but the Spirit who is from God, that we might know the things that have been freely given to us by God" (1 Cor. 2:12).

Paul and John also wrote about a pervasive spirit that characterizes evil people. In Ephesians 2:2 we read about the "prince of the power of the air, the spirit who now works in the sons of disobedience." John refers to "false prophets"—those who are spokespersons for what is evil (1 John 4:1). Peter said, "There were also false prophets among the people, even as there will be false teachers among you, who will secretly bring in destructive heresies, even denying the Lord who bought them, and bring on themselves swift destruction" (2 Peter 2:1).

These people who operate with an evil intent and speak things contrary to the will of God are operating in the spirit of antichrist. Everything they say is opposed to Christ and everything they do is an attempt to take over the place that is rightfully Christ's alone.

• *Have you ever encountered a person who operated in the spirit of antichrist? How did you feel in that person's presence?*

_____

_____

Our Responsibility to Test the Spirits

Jesus warned His disciples that there would be people who would attempt to deceive the believers:

> *Take heed that no one deceives you. For many will come in My name, saying, "I am the Christ," and will deceive many. . . . false christs and false prophets will rise and show great signs and wonders to deceive, if possible, even the elect. (Matt. 24:4–5, 24)*

Paul also warned against those who would preach any gospel other than the gospel of Christ. He spoke of "false apostles, deceitful workers, transforming themselves into apostles of Christ" (2 Cor. 11:13).

We are warned repeatedly throughout the Scriptures that we are never to accept a person's message as being true on the basis of that person's personality, appearance, or ability to communicate, or on the basis of the number of people who follow him, the music or testimonials he presents, or the promises he makes. The only basis for our acceptance of any person's teaching and testimony must be this: it is in complete agreement with the written Word of God.

We are to *test* the spirits against the criterion of God's Word, and specifically against the criterion of what is said about Jesus in God's Word. Any person who says that Jesus Christ is not God's Son come in the flesh, or who denies the sovereignty of Christ as the sole and complete provision for salvation, is false. (See 1 John 4:1–3.)

We also must be on guard that we do not buy into a person's teaching or testimony because the person seems to be speaking the truth about one particular issue or concern. We must consider always the "whole counsel" of God's Word—*everything* that a person says must be in line with God's Word, not just a portion of what he says.

What the Word Says	What the Word Says to Me
Beloved, do not believe every spirit, but test the spirits, whether they are of God; because many false prophets have gone out into the world. By this you know the Spirit of God: Every spirit that confesses that Jesus Christ has come in the flesh is of God, and every spirit that does not confess that Jesus Christ has come in the flesh is not of God. And this is the spirit of the Antichrist, which you have heard was coming, and is now already in the world (1 John 4:1–3).	--------------------------------- --------------------------------- --------------------------------- --------------------------------- --------------------------------- --------------------------------- --------------------------------- --------------------------------- --------------------------------- --------------------------------- --------------------------------- --------------------------------- ---------------------------------
For I have not shunned to declare to you the whole counsel of God. Therefore take heed to yourselves. . . . For I know this, that after my departure savage wolves will come in among you, not sparing the flock. Also from among yourselves men will rise up, speaking perverse things, to draw away the disciples after themselves (Acts 20:27–30).	--------------------------------- --------------------------------- --------------------------------- --------------------------------- --------------------------------- --------------------------------- --------------------------------- --------------------------------- --------------------------------- ---------------------------------

- *In what ways are you being challenged in your spirit?*

Characteristics of Those with False Spirits

Those who are filled with the spirit of antichrist, the devil's own spirit, often have the following characteristics:

1. They are manipulative. False teachers exploit others and use others for their own gain. If allowed to amass power, they will seek to drain all of the finances of those who follow them. They seek to destroy the individuality of their followers, often requiring that their followers dress and act in highly prescribed ways.

2. They promote sensuality. False teachers nearly always claim that sensuality is to be highly valued and sexual sins are permissible. Many cult leaders are advocates and practitioners of blatant fornication and adultery.

3. They secretly introduce destructive heresies. They take a portion of God's Word and twist it into a form that seems reasonable and palatable to human lusts and desires. They hold out a principle about which men can say, "Yes, that's the way it *ought* to be." The trouble is, the principle they proclaim is not what the Word of God holds to be truth. For example, false teachers today proclaim that there are many ways to approach God and experience salvation. People clamor after this heresy, saying, "Surely God wouldn't send a person to hell for not believing in Christ." The Bible says that Jesus is *the* way, *the* truth, *the* life, and that nobody comes to the Father but by Him (John 14:6).

4. They exhibit personal materialism and greed. False teachers with an antichrist spirit nearly always surround themselves with great wealth. Peter said, "By covetousness they will exploit you with deceptive words" (2 Peter 2:3).

- *Have you or someone you know been the victim of a person who is filled with an antichrist spirit?*

_____

_____

The Outcome for Those with an Antichrist Spirit

The Scriptures give us a fivefold progression related to those who have an antichrist spirit. This progression is most evident in the life of the future antichrist world leader, called the Beast, but it is also the path that is followed by any person who allows himself to be filled with Satan's spirit.

First, the person displays lawlessness. The person with an antichrist spirit has no regard for God's law. To the contrary, he ridicules God's law as he dismisses its value. Those with an antichrist spirit also hold themselves to be above the laws that govern other people. They have little regard for order or justice. They rule according to their own whims and dictates. Paul wrote to the church at Thessalonica:

> The mystery of lawlessness is already at work; only He who now restrains will do so until He is taken out of the way. . . . The coming of the lawless one is according to the working of Satan, with all power, signs, and lying wonders. (2 Thess. 2:7, 9)

Second, the person claims to be a deity. He claims special powers or wisdom. Just as Satan before him, he claims to have knowledge about God that God hasn't revealed to others. At times, the person will claim to be under God but on par with Jesus—the mind-set is usually that Jesus was just a good man, a prophet, and that there are and have been many such people, the person making the claim among them. False prophets claim that Jesus was only *a* son of God, not *the* Son, and that people today can have as much authority and dominion as Jesus. While we are called to become sons and daughters of God and joint heirs with Christ, we are always under Christ's authority. The Bible never claims that any person can do what Christ did or be what Christ is—the only begotten Son of God, the Savior of the world, the Lord of lords and King of kings forevermore.

Paul addressed these lies directly: "There is no other God but one. . . . there is one God, the Father, of whom are all things, and we for Him; and one Lord Jesus Christ, through whom are all things, and through whom we live" (1 Cor. 8:4, 6).

Third, the person seeks to rule others. People who are filled with an antichrist spirit do not live in isolation. They recruit followers and build power structures. They long to manipulate, control, and rule over people, places, and things. Their desire for power over other people is insatiable, although their outward demeanor may be one of false humility and gentleness.

Jesus taught us to pray to our heavenly Father, "Yours is the kingdom and the power and the glory forever" (Matt. 6:13). Anybody who attempts to get you to ascribe to his or her absolute rulership, power, and glory is a person with an antichrist spirit.

Fourth, the person is a tool of Satan. The person may appear to be the one doing the ruling and teaching, but ultimately, he is a pawn in the hands of Satan. Satan gives a form of power to his followers, but it is the power described in Revelation 9:3: "To them was given power, as the scorpions of the earth have power." This is the power to sting, to inflict pain, to cause suffering, to bring about loss, destruction, and devastation.

Jesus taught, "Whoever commits sin is a slave of sin" (John 8:34). The person with an antichrist spirit may *think* he is acting of his own accord; in reality he is a victim of Satan.

Fifth, the person is ultimately destroyed by God. God may allow a person with an antichrist spirit to exert influence for a season, but the person with this spirit is ultimately removed from the scene by God. Paul wrote, "What fruit did you have then in the things of which you are now ashamed? For the end of those things is death. . . . the wages of sin is death, but the gift of God is eternal life in Christ Jesus our Lord" (Rom. 6:21, 23).

Nothing built by a person with an antichrist spirit survives for very long. False religions come and go. Cults based on false teachings rise and fall. Empires built by people with antichrist spirits crumble. Only what is of Christ lasts on this earth. Only those whom Christ redeems will live forever.

- *What new insights do you have into the nature of our enemy and how to overcome him?*

_____

_____

Three Questions to Ask

If you believe you are facing a person who has a false spirit, there are three questions you should ask:

1. What do you believe about Jesus? Was He God? A person with an antichrist spirit will hem and haw at the question. The person who is a true Christian will say, "Jesus was God come in the flesh." John said, "Every spirit that does not confess that Jesus Christ has come in the flesh is not of God" (1 John 4:3).

2. What do you believe about humankind and about humans' relationship to God? A person with an antichrist spirit will claim that humankind is supreme; God is a nice idea that is valuable to people, but in the end, God is humankind's creation. Others with an antichrist spirit will claim that God exists to serve people. The true Christian will say, "Humankind is valuable to God, but humankind is always subservient to God. Humankind's role is to serve God."

A person with an antichrist spirit will claim that humankind has no need for salvation, and that if humankind desires to improve itself, it is capable of doing so without any help from God. The true Christian will say, "People need salvation and are incapable of earning it or achieving it on their own. Salvation is a gift of God, freely made available through Jesus Christ to all who will believe."

3. What do you believe about the Bible? A person with a spirit of antichrist will be opposed to hearing the Word of God and will have no interest in the things of God. He will dismiss the Bible's authenticity and authority. He will be opposed to any efforts that a person makes to live a life in accordance with God's commandments.

The true Christian will say, "I believe the Bible to be the authoritative Word of God, good for instruction. It presents the way that God desires for me to live, think, feel, and believe."

When we ask these questions of a person, we must listen closely to the answers with spiritual ears. We must ask the Holy Spirit to alert us to anything that is contrary to God's Word. We can trust the Holy Spirit to prick our consciences so that we will be able to tell right from wrong. John said, "By this we know the spirit of truth and the spirit of error" (1 John 4:6).

What the Word Says	What the Word Says to Me
And you He made alive, who were dead in trespasses and sins, in which you once walked according to the course of this world . . . among whom also we all once	

conducted ourselves in the lusts of our flesh, fulfilling the desires of the flesh and of the mind, and were by nature children of wrath, just as the others. But God, who is rich in mercy, because of His great love with which He loved us, even when we were dead in trespasses, made us alive together with Christ (by grace you have been saved), and raised us up together, and made us sit together in the heavenly places in Christ Jesus, that in the ages to come He might show the exceeding riches of His grace in His kindness toward us in Christ Jesus (Eph. 2:1–7).

For by grace you have been saved through faith, and that not of yourselves; it is the gift of God, not of works, lest anyone should boast (Eph. 2:8–9).

Every word of God is pure;
He is a shield to those who put their trust in Him.
Do not add to His words,
Lest He rebuke you, and you be found a liar (Prov. 30:5–6).

By this we know that we abide in Him, and He in us, because He has given us of His Spirit (1 John 4:13).

Pervasive but Not Unbeatable

The spirit of antichrist is pervasive in our world today, but it can be confronted, challenged, and denied. We do not need to be victims of those who are operating according to Satan's dictates or who are filled with his spirit. We *can* overcome the enemy if we will be committed to a persistent, unrelenting search for and compliance with God's truth.

- *In what ways are you being challenged in your spirit?*

_____

_____

LESSON 10

CHOOSING FAITH OVER REASON AND EMOTION

When faced with any decision or choice in life, we operate from one of three positions: faith, reason, or emotion. Faith flows from the spirit of a man or woman. God endows us with faith so we can make right choices related to Him. Reason and emotion flow from the soul of man—from what we often term the mind and the heart. Man experiences thoughts and feelings in his soul.

Thoughts and feelings are not eternal. They are related directly to the information, perceptions, and physical sensations we have at a moment in time. Because of this, our thoughts and feelings can vary widely, according to time and circumstances. We often have competing thoughts and feelings, and we base our thoughts and feelings to a great extent on the thoughts and feelings of others who are close to us.

Faith says in the face of a situation, "This is what God says."

Reason says, "This is what I think and what seems right to me."

Emotion says, "This is how I feel right now and I am going to go with my feelings and do what feels good."

Faith, reason, and emotion are all related, of course. It's virtually impossible to separate them at times. But what we are concerned about in dealing with the devil is the fact that the devil never appeals to our faith. He only appeals to our reason and emotions. Furthermore, he attempts at all times to drive a wedge between faith and reason/emotions.

When we honor and obey God in a situation, God works to bring our reason and emotions in line with our faith. When we obey the devil, we are fragmented and confused.

God Values Reason and Emotion

God is not opposed to reason, or to our using our minds or expressing our feelings. Quite the contrary. God desires for us to be reasonable and emotionally healthy people. God's laws are extremely reasonable and logical. When a person fully obeys God's laws he or she experiences great joy.

What God desires is that we reason *with* Him, not apart from Him. In fact, the Scriptures tell us He invites us to reason with Him: "Come now, and let us reason together" (Isa. 1:18). The very next verse describes the consequences to obedience and disobedience in this matter:

> *If you are willing and obedient,*
> *You shall eat the good of the land;*
> *But if you refuse and rebel,*
> *You shall be devoured by the sword.* (Isa. 1:19–20)

God very much wants us to understand that His thoughts, plans, and methods are greater than anything we could imagine:

> *My thoughts are not your thoughts,*
> *Nor are your ways My ways. . . .*
> *For as the heavens are higher than the earth,*
> *So are My ways higher than your ways,*
> *And My thoughts than your thoughts.* (Isa. 55:8–9)

No matter how much we know about a particular issue or situation, we cannot know as much as God knows about it. As much as we might love another person and desire good on his or her behalf, we cannot love that person as much as God does. When we rely on our human emotions and reasoning ability, rather than submitting these to God and responding with our faith, we shortchange ourselves. And the devil delights anytime we deny God, ignore God, or fail to experience God's best.

- *Can you cite an experience in your life in which you discovered that God's plan, methods, or blessing was different and greater than anything you had imagined or anticipated?*

_____

The First Faith vs. Reason Conflict

The first instance in which we see faith and reason in conflict in the Scriptures is in the Garden of Eden. Satan, in the guise of a beautiful and cunning serpent, came to Eve and said, "Has God indeed said, 'You shall not eat of every tree of the garden'?" And Eve replied, "We may eat the fruit of the trees of the garden; but of the fruit of the tree which is in the midst of the garden, God has said, 'You shall not eat it, nor shall you touch it, lest you die.'" The serpent told Eve, "You will not surely die. For God knows that in the day you eat of it your eyes will be opened, and you will be like God, knowing good and evil." (See Gen. 3:1–5.)

Satan appealed to Eve's reasoning ability. He introduced doubt—perhaps God didn't really mean what He had said; or perhaps God was holding out on Eve and not giving her everything that was for her good.

Eve made a decision based on her reasoning ability, not on her faith in God. Throughout history, we have continued to make Eve's mistake.

- *Can you cite instances in which you have made important decisions based on reason or emotion, rather than on faith?*

_____

_____

Accepting and Obeying God's Absolutes

The world that Satan governs has no tolerance for God's absolutes. Consider these four issues:

- Prayer in schools
- Abortion policies
- Sexual identity
- Financial debt

In each of these areas, people argue ardently from both reason and emotion. These highly volatile issues generate all manner of opinions and feelings in people. Answers, decisions, and public policies often are made on the basis of intellectual, "logical" reasoning. Individual decisions and attitudes very often are rooted in the way a person feels about the issue. People can argue all facets of these issues, and usually the more they argue their position, the more heated they become in their expression.

The alternative is to ask, "What does God say?"

What does the Bible say about prayer? Is it good? Is it good for children? Is it appropriately applied to learning?

What does the Bible say about taking innocent human life? What does the Bible say about bearing children and nurturing them in godly principles? What does the Bible say about fornication, incest, and rape?

What does the Bible say about homosexual behavior?

What does the Bible say about borrowing and lending?

The biblical views on most issues of life are nearly always simple, straightforward, and easy to understand. God's commandments are not shrouded in mystery. Even a young child can understand the Ten Commandments. The problem is not that we don't know God's opinion. The problem is that we don't want to obey what God says to do and not do.

Anytime we know what to do and then fail to do it, we are in rebellion against God. That is a very dangerous position.

What the Word Says

What the Word Says to Me

The law of the LORD is perfect,
converting the soul;
The testimony of the LORD is sure,
making wise the simple;
The statutes of the LORD are right,
rejoicing the heart;
The commandment of the LORD is
pure, enlightening the eyes;
The fear of the LORD is clean,
enduring forever;
The judgments of the LORD are
true and righteous altogether.
More to be desired are they
than gold,
Yea, than much fine gold;
Sweeter also than honey and the
honeycomb.
Moreover by them Your servant
is warned,
And in keeping them there is great
reward (Ps. 19:7–11).

Say now to the rebellious house:
"Do you not know what these
things mean?" . . . But he rebelled
against him. . . . Will he prosper?
Will he who does such things
escape? Can he break a covenant
and still be delivered?" (Ezek.
17:12, 15).

Do not rebel against the LORD, nor
fear the people of the land (Num.
14:9).

Whether it is pleasing or displeas-
ing, we will obey the voice of the
LORD our God . . . that it may be

----

well with us when we obey the
voice of the LORD our God (Jer.
42:6).

Faith Is the Only Way to Know God

When Paul wrote to the Corinthians, he was writing to Greeks who held reasoning and logic in very high regard. They were specialists in "the wisdom of man." The message of the Cross made no sense to them. Paul said to them:

> For the message of the cross is foolishness to those who are perishing, but to us who are being saved it is the power of God. For it is written: "I will destroy the wisdom of the wise, / And bring to nothing the understanding of the prudent." Where is the wise? Where is the scribe? Where is the disputer of this age? Has not God made foolish the wisdom of this world? . . . The foolishness of God is wiser than men, and the weakness of God is stronger than men. (1 Cor. 1:18–20, 25)

Reasoning is not the way we come to know God or to understand Him. Why? Because the human mind cannot comprehend God. All false religions assume otherwise. They believe that if you only hone the intellect so that it is sharp enough, then you can analyze and understand God. They subject the intellect to a performance criterion.

Every false religious system or cult is based on performance—on meeting certain standards. A person is told what to do, for how long, and to what degree. None of it works. Why? Because when you are facing an infinite, omniscient, omnipotent God, how can you possibly know when you have done enough, know enough, or have achieved enough? There is no way a finite creature with a finite brain can know or calculate the expectations of an infinite God.

Only by faith can we come to understand God—in other words, when we *believe* that God is just and righteous and merciful and loving and forgiving *solely* on the basis that this is what He said about Himself. Faith is believing that God has resources and evidence that we can't know, don't know, and may never know.

To a person who is attempting to find a logical way to God, the Cross is not going to make any sense at all. To the person who hopes to "feel" his or her way into God's presence, the Cross is going to be repulsive. And yet this is the means that God has chosen for the redemption of humankind. We must believe in God and believe that God knows best, not only for us but for every other person.

God's Illogical Methods

God's laws and commandments are highly logical. God's methods very often are not. Consider these possibilities:

• In facing a major battle against a formidable foe, an army commander is told to have his troops circle a city once a day for six days, and then circle it seven times on the seventh day, after which the troops are to blow trumpets and shout. The commander obeys and so do the troops. When the trumpets are sounded and the shouts are voiced, the walls of the city tumble and a victory is won.

• A leader is faced with a difficult situation. He has led thousands upon thousands of people out into a wilderness area. Now, in front of him is a sea of water. Approaching his people from the rear are the most powerful forces of Pharaoh, which are intent upon capturing the people and returning them to slavery. God tells the leader to put his rod into the water. He does so. The people walk across on dry ground.

• A young wife is facing a death sentence and opts to fast and pray, and then to host two dinner parties for her husband and her archenemy. In the course of the second dinnertime conversation, she openly accuses her enemy, and in the end her own life is spared, along with the lives of her people.

• Three young leaders are told that they must bow to a statue that has been built by the emperor they serve. They are told that if they refuse they will be thrown into a fiery furnace. They refuse, nonetheless, and God allows them to be thrown into the furnace. They live through the experience, coming out of the furnace without even the smell of smoke on their clothes.

Do any of these situations make any intellectual sense? No! They are contrary to logic and reasoning.

Do any of these situations make sense in light of normal emotional responses? No! The normal emotional response would be to cave in to fear and seek an alternative plan.

By faith, however, Joshua, Moses, Esther, and Shadrach, Meshach, and Abed-Nego scored mighty victories that brought glory to God. What God asked them to do—march around a city and shout, put a rod into the water, prepare a couple of banquets, and be thrown into a fiery furnace—was highly illogical and against normal human emotional response. Actions based solely on faith, however, brought about good results for God's people and the elimination of God's enemies.

What the Word Says	What the Word Says to Me
Jesus said to him, "If you can believe, all things are possible to him who believes." Immediately the father of the child cried out and said with tears, "Lord, I believe; help my unbelief!" (Mark 9:23–24).	
He who believes and is baptized will be saved; but he who does not believe will be condemned (Mark 16:16).	
Therefore let it be known to you, brethren, that through this Man is preached to you the forgiveness of sins; and by Him everyone who believes is justified from all things from which you could not be justified by the law of Moses (Acts 13:38–39).	

Refuse to Be Blinded

When we seek to understand God through reason alone, our reasoning efforts blind us to God. Paul wrote:

> *If our gospel is veiled, it is veiled to those who are perishing, whose minds the god of this age has blinded, who do not believe, lest the light of the gospel of the glory of Christ, who is the image of God, should shine on them. (2 Cor. 4:3–4)*

As long as we demand that logic be followed, we cannot accept much of the Bible, for it simply does not make sense to us. Nobody can pull this blindfold from our eyes. Each of us must come to the conclusion for ourselves: "Lord, I believe, help my unbelief." We are incapable of seeing the fullness of God's truth until we take this first step.

- *In what ways are you feeling challenged in your spirit?*

No Excuses

The devil continually tempts us to justify our sins and to reason away our faith. He constantly entices us to respond to our emotions— especially fear, anger, and hatred—rather than to respond with faith. Don't listen to him! Choose to respond with your faith.

When you respond with faith in Jesus Christ, you put your adversary on the run.

- *What new insights do you have into your adversary and how to overcome him?*

CONCLUSION

ENJOIN THE BATTLE

The very mention of the devil's name evokes fear in many people. For others, the devil seems to be a joke.

As Christians, we are to take the devil seriously, but we are not to be overwhelmed by him or give in to his temptations. We are not to ignore him or dismiss him lightly, but rather, we are to face him, resist him, and use our faith to overcome him.

We can take this stance only if we remain close to Christ Jesus, turn to the Holy Spirit daily for wisdom, courage, and direction, and above all, choose to believe what Christ has said to us: we *are* God's forgiven children and the devil has no claim on our eternal spirits.

Others may pray for us, believe with us, and encourage us in our battle against the enemy—all to our benefit—but in the end, we cannot hide behind the faith of others. Facing the devil is something each of us must do if we are to grow in our relationship with God. Facing the devil exercises our personal faith. It is an act of personal obedience to God. We must be *willing* to face the enemy of our souls if we are to be in a position to receive all the blessings and rewards that God has for us.

In Christ Jesus, you *can* and *will* overcome the enemy. Engage in the battle. Trust God today for a victorious life!